MEMORIES

Derbyshire Coalfields

David Bell

COUNTRYSIDE BOOKS
NEWBURY BERKSHIRE

First published 2006
© David Bell 2006

COUNTRYSIDE BOOKS
3 Catherine Road
Newbury, Berkshire

To view our complete range of books,
please visit us at
www.countrysidebooks.co.uk

ISBN 1 84674 003 7
EAN 978 1 84674 003 9

Designed by Peter Davies, Nautilus Design

Produced through MRM Associates Ltd., Reading
Typeset by CJWT Solutions, Newton-le-Willows
Printed by Woolnough Bookbinding Ltd., Irthlingborough

Contents

Acknowledgements

I wish to thank the following individuals for their help in writing this book: Roy Astle, Gary Bacon, John Burrows, Walter Burrows, Terry Butkeraitis, Kathrine Durkan, Austin Fairest, Keith Foster, Ruth Gordon, Lee Harper, Ron Harvey, Monica Hudson, Paul Liversuch, Betty Mappley, Graham Nutt, Henry Richardson, Dennis Skinner, Sherryl Stansbury, Ron Wain, Eric Walton and Cliff Williams.

I would also like to acknowledge help given by the local studies section of Derbyshire Library HQ in Matlock, Swadlincote library, Clause IV in Worksop, South Derbyshire Mining Preservation Group, Magic Attic Archives, People Express, CPL Distribution, and Sharpe's Pottery Heritage & Arts Trust Ltd.

MAP OF THE DERBYSHIRE COALFIELDS

MAP A: Working pits in north-east Derbyshire in 1955

High Moor
West Thorpe
Renishaw Park•
Whitwell
Ireland• Oxcroft
Markham• Cresswell
CHESTERFIELD■ •Bolsover •Langwith
Arkwright
Williamthorpe Ramcroft Shirebrook
Holmwood• •Glapwell
•Parkhouse •Pleasley
Woolley Moor •Pilsley
•Morton
Shirland •Blackwell Winning
Wingfield •Alfreton
Manor • •Cotes Park
Swanwick

New Langley
Woodside•
•Stanley

MAP B: Working pits in south Derbyshire in 1955

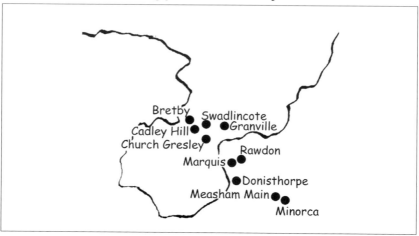

Bretby Swadlincote
Cadley Hill •Granville
Church Gresley
Rawdon
Marquis•
•Donisthorpe
Measham Main•
Minorca

6

Introduction

In 1994, when Markham colliery on the North Derbyshire coalfield closed, coal mining in Derbyshire came to an end and a way of life familiar to generations of miners and their families disappeared forever. There are still many former miners in the county, however, all with fascinating and sometimes moving tales to tell of life above and below ground, and it is their stories that form the basis of this book.

Mining had taken place in Derbyshire for many centuries. There is a medieval carving of a miner known as 't'owd man' in Wirksworth church – though he was a lead miner rather than a collier. However, there is a reference in 1789 to the 'amazing' number of pits around Staunton Harold, where 'the land itself is as black as if the coal lay above ground'. The pits there were obviously even older because in the early 14th century, action had been taken against Sir William Staunton of Staunton Hall for not paying tithes on his mineral products, named as iron and coal. Two charters of 1374 and 1377 indicate that coal was being mined at Swadlincote, and as early as 1204, the freemen of Swannington were granted the right 'to mine coal on the common'. Further north, it is well established that coal was being extracted in the Swanwick/Alfreton area in the 13th century.

Derbyshire had two coalfields, one in the north-east of the county, lying between Chesterfield and the county border with Nottinghamshire, the other, in the south, in the area around the town of Swadlincote. Both stretched into other counties. The larger, northern one extended east into Nottinghamshire and north into Yorkshire, while it will be noted from the map that as well as pits at Granville, Church Gresley, Stanhope Drift, Bretby, Swadlincote, and Cadley Hill, the South Derbyshire area also

An iconic sight lost to Derbyshire – the headstock at Ireland colliery before closure in 1987. (John Burrows)

included mines that were geographically in Leicestershire. This anomaly occurred because the division between the South Derbyshire coalfield and the Leicestershire coalfield did not coincide with the county boundary, but was dictated by a subterranean feature, the Boothorpe Fault. The two pits in Measham, the two at Moira (Rawdon and Marquis), and Donisthorpe colliery were traditionally recognised by both sides of the industry – the Coal Board and the unions – as part of the South Derbyshire coalfield.

It was the canals that enabled the heavy coal to be transported over great distances, and the building of the Chesterfield canal in the north of the county and the Ashby canal in the south led to a great expansion of coal mining. Later, the coming of the railways increased production even more. By 1840, Derbyshire coal was being sent to London and to all parts of the country in ever increasing quantities. By 1906, Derbyshire's 176 pits were producing 16,250,000 tons of coal.

Not only was there an increase in coal mining but, where iron ore was brought up with the coal, iron foundries grew up, for

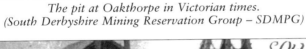

The pit at Oakthorpe in Victorian times.
(South Derbyshire Mining Reservation Group – SDMPG)

9

Cadley Hill pit in the 1920s. (Magic Attic Archives)

example, at Staveley and at Ironville. Where clay was found, pottery firms became established. One such was at Denby, and the whole area around Swadlincote became known for its pottery products. The firm of TG Green at Woodville is famous for its blue and white 'Cornish ware', and Measham bargeware teapots were another renowned local product. At Swadlincote, the kilns of Sharpe's Pottery produced domestic items and also sanitary ware for both the UK and the USA. This former pottery now houses a museum, as well as a local history archive and a community arts organisation. Other clay products ranged from the ceramic works of Bretby Art Pottery to household bricks, which are still manufactured in the area.

Throughout the 19th and first half of the 20th centuries, Derbyshire pits closed when they ran out of coal, and new ones were opened. In 1955, there were still ten coal mines in the South Derbyshire coalfield and more than 30 in the north of the county, including Markham colliery. Walter Burrows, who worked there for 40 years as a face worker, then as a shot firer and later as a deputy, told me, 'Markham was the biggest colliery in the country, the biggest in the whole of Europe.' He started work there in 1950: 'There were 3,000 lockers at Markham but I had to share my dad's for a couple of years, because there were far more than 3,000 men. Most collieries only had two or three working faces, but Markham was so big it had ten working faces at one time.'

Following the 1984-85 national miners' strike, the picture changed. The government and Coal Board had planned to start a massive programme of pit closures and many miners saw this as an attempt to punish them for bringing down the government of Ted Heath in 1972, and to prepare a much smaller mining industry for eventual privatisation. The importance of the strike to the men and women whose lives were bound up with the working of the mines is fully reflected in the memories that are recorded here.

The strike was supported with great enthusiasm in north Derbyshire, though not in the south of the county, but afterwards mines throughout Derbyshire were closed down. Measham and Whitwell pits were shut in 1986, and Ireland the following year. Two more, Cadley Hill and Arkwright, were closed in 1988, and in 1989 Renishaw Park and Rawdon both went. This left just one pit, Donisthorpe, working in South Derbyshire, but that pit was terminated in 1990. In the north Derbyshire coalfield, Bolsover and Shirebrook went in 1993. Because High Moor had been transferred to the Yorkshire area in 1990, this left Markham pit the last colliery in Derbyshire, until it, too, closed in 1994.

Many ex-miners agreed to share their memories of pit work with me, talking about the conditions in which they worked, the laughs they had with their fellow-miners, and the accidents – some minor and some major – that they experienced.

David Bell

11

DERBYSHIRE COLLIERIES AND MINERS IN 1955

NORTH-EAST COALFIELD

Westthorpe   1,266 men
  (1,058 underground &
  208 surface)

Renishaw Park   676 men
  (578 & 98)

Ireland   1,253 men (1,022 & 231)

Markham no 1, 2 and 4   3,001 men
  (2,427 & 574)

Arkwright   695 men (580 & 115)

Bolsover   1,029 men (829 & 200)

Oxcroft   747 men (635 & 112)

Whitwell   1,194 men (985 & 209)

Cresswell   1,371 men (1071 & 300)

Langwith   1,240 men (984 & 256)

Ramcroft   538 men (437 & 101)

Shirebrook   1,590 men
  (1,232 & 358)

Glapwell no 1 and 3   2,675 men
  (2,188 & 487)

Pleasley   1,360 men (1,038 & 322)

Williamthorpe and Grassmoor
  2,607 men (2,191 & 416)

Holmewood   1,301 men
  (974 & 327)

Parkhouse   883 men (744 & 139)

Pilsley   405 men (330 & 75)

Morton   956 men (814 & 142)

Shirland   469 men (354 & 115)

Blackwell 'A' and 'B' Winning
  1,746 men (1,452 & 294)

Alfreton   948 men (756 & 192)

Wingfield Manor   613 men
  (495 & 118)

Cotes Park   391 men (323 & 68)

Swanwick   1,164 men (962 & 202)

New Langley   476 men (396 & 80)

Woodside   1,664 men
  (1,359 & 305)

SOUTH COALFIELD

Bretby   447 men (345 & 102)

Cadley Hill   497 men (378 & 119)

Swadlincote 557 men (427 & 130)

Church Gresley   974 men
  (748 & 226)

Granville   694 men (533 & 161)

Rawdon and Marquis   1196 men
  (969 & 227)

Donisthorpe   1140 men
  (925 & 215)

Measham and Minorca   698 men
  (558 & 140)

THE LIFE SPAN OF THE POST-WAR DERBYSHIRE PITS

Britain	1918-1946	Alfreton	1886-1968
Netherseal	1855-1947	Denby	1839-1968
Reservoir	1851-1948	Swanwick	1866-1968
Ripley	1863-1948	Holmewood	1870-1968
Bonds Main	1897-1949	A Winning	1872-1969
Manners	1877-1949	Ormonde	1908-1970
Grassmoor	1875-1950	Bramley Vale	1959-1970
Pilsley	1865-1957	Williamthorpe	1905-1970
Wooley Moor Drift	1954-1958	Oxcroft	1949-1974
New Langley	1959-1960	Glapwell	1882-1974
Stanley	1903-1961	Langwith	1878-1978
Woodside 2 & 3	1899-1961	Pleasley	1871-1983
Bretby	1872-1962	Westthorpe	1924-1984
Parkhouse	1866-1962	Measham	1850-1986
Cotes Park	1850-1963	Whitwell	1890-1986
Wingfield Manor	1906-1964	Ireland	1858-1987
B Winning	1874-1964	Cadley Hill	1860-1988
Morton	1863-1963	Arkwright	1899-1988
Shirland	1864-1965	Rawdon	1821-1989
Swadlincote	1852-1965	Renishaw Park	1860-1989
Mapperley	1872-1965	Warsop	1895-1989
Stanhope Drift	1959-1966	Donisthorpe	1871-1990
Ramcroft	1916-1966	Bolsover	1891-1993
Woodside No 1	1948-1966	Shirebrook	1897-1993
Coppice	1875-1966	Markham	1882-1994
Church Gresley	1812-1967	High Moor	1953-1995
Granville	1823-1967		

Chapter 1

Life in a Mining Community

ife in a mining town or village had a special feel to it and the miners and their families lived, worked and relaxed in a tightly-knit community.

Many of these communities supported a wide variety of sporting and other social activities. There is a legend that if Derbyshire County Cricket Club ever needed a new fast bowler they'd just shout down the nearest pit and the first man who came up would do, because all the miners had such powerful shoulders. Many pits also had football teams. Joe Payne, who died in 1975, had turned out for his Bolsover Colliery team before going on to play as a professional footballer at Luton Town, Chelsea and West Ham, gaining his cap for England in 1937. He achieved lasting fame as 'Ten Goal Payne', and still holds the record as the only man in league football to score ten goals in one match. Dennis Skinner, who has been the Labour MP for Bolsover since 1970 and who worked down Parkhouse Colliery at Clay Cross and later at Glapwell pit, was another miner who took full advantage of the sporting activities available, taking up cycling, athletics, football, cricket and tennis.

Some collieries – Cresswell, Ireland, Church Gresley and Moira were among them – had their own brass bands, although in the early days, according to Clay Cross historian Cliff Williams, those miners who played in the bands were often regarded as *flunkeys* (bosses' men), who got extra privileges at work. However, I'm sure that those men who played in the bands in more recent times, plus their families and friends, would think that a harsh judgement. One exciting thing about the colliery bands was that they took part in competitions, and often the coach taking a local band to such exotic places as Blackpool would be packed with supporters, keen for their colliery band to outplay those from other areas.

Miners loved any hobby that involved competing, whether it was growing enormous leeks or breeding whippets and racing pigeons. The miners' pigeons would be sent to another location and all released together for the race home. When the pigeon got home to its owner's pigeon loft, the man would take off its tab. This had to be put into a machine to register the time of its arrival,

South Derbyshire Miners (Gresley) Brass Band. (Magic Attic Archives)

The men who played in the early brass bands were sometimes seen as 'flunkeys', or bosses' men, by their fellow miners. (Magic Attic Archives)

Travelling to competitions was a treat for both the band and its supporters; this is Gresley Colliery Silver Band outside Blackpool Opera House in the late 1970s. (Magic Attic Archives)

*Pit ponies at Cadley Hill in 1911 – these two had won third prize
at Ashby Show. (Magic Attic Archives)*

but because the machine was an expensive piece of kit, it was kept
in the local pub. The landlord was in charge of seeing fair play. So
once your pigeon was back, you would hurry to the pub with the
tab. If you lived near the pub, or if you had a bike, or if you were
a young man with a good turn of speed, that was an advantage.
As Cliff Williams explained, it wasn't always the fastest pigeon
that won: it was the pigeon whose owner could get to the pub the
quickest!

Betty Mapwell grew up in Station Road, Bolsover, next door to
the Nag's Head pub. Her father, John Thompson, worked at
Glapwell pit and she recalls: 'I remember my dad coming home
black every day, he never used the pit baths. We'd got a very
large coalhouse, coal at one end and the other end was where my
mother did her washing. There was a big stone boiler, and the
bath was in there. So my dad had his bath in the coalhouse! It

Crowie Peters of Clay Cross, with his racing pigeons. (Cliff Williams)

was hot in there because you'd got the fire under the boiler. That's one thing we'd always got – plenty of coal. It was in big lumps and he used to have to bash them up. Then at night he'd put a huge lump on the fire, because we had a black range, and the fire was still in next morning. The porridge was always put in the oven in a stew pot.

'He had a tradition of getting ready for work. He come downstairs with his trousers on, then he'd tie string round the bottom of each leg. I think it was to stop the dirt getting in, to keep his legs clean. The trousers were made out of some sort of skin, and they used to go very hard. My mother had a job washing them. He had a shirt with no collar, as I remember, but he had one of those white silk scarves. It used to come round his neck, and he fastened it through his braces, and tied it at the front. He always wore that to work. It probably got a bit grubby but it'd get washed every week. I don't know whether he wore it while he was working. All I remember is, it was on when he went off to work and on when he came back.

'I remember his snap tin and his water bottle, which in north Derbyshire was called a *dudley*, but they don't know that name in the south Derbyshire pits. At the miners' club, the men down here didn't know what I meant when I mentioned a dudley. I told them it was a metal water can. The snap tin was metal too, to keep the mice out. Dad smoked a pipe but he didn't smoke pipe tobacco in it, he smoked chewing tobacco. He'd scrape it with his nail into flakes. He used to buy a screw of chewing tobacco.

'There was our house, then a pub next door, and the other side of the pub was Mr Ford's grocery shop. My mum used to work for him, cleaning. I remember once I'd gone for some prunes. You know a grocer's shop in the olden days, the man stood there and he'd got his tins all on the front of the counter, with lids on. He just lifted the lid and filled your bag. Anyway, Mr Ford served me with some prunes. My mother used to soak them and we'd have them with custard. Come teatime, I'd got a bowl of prunes and custard, and I was eating what I thought was a prune, and it turned out to be a screw of tobacco. And that put me off – I've

The Miners Arms at Brimington, at the heart of a mining community.

never touched a prune since. I can't look at a prune now. I think of that day when I'd got a piece of tobacco in my mouth. The man must have been giving somebody some 'baccy, and they never used to wrap things up, did they? If you bought a screw of 'baccy, you got it in your hand, and obviously he'd dropped it in the prunes.'

A lot of miners chewed tobacco because they couldn't smoke down the pit, though even chewing it could lead to accidents. Ron Harvey, who trained at the Central Workshops in Swadlincote as an apprentice fitter and then worked at Gresley colliery, told me, 'I've seen 'em once lose nearly a whole shift of coal through chewing tobacco. Peter Grice used to drive the coal cutting machine at Gresley pit, and they'd got no back-up driver, and he was chewing this tobacco. The machine hit some hard coal and gave a lurch and he swallowed the tobacco, and he had to go out, he was that ill. And until they sent a replacement, the face stood idle.'

Betty Mapley continues: 'We were very poor in some respects, but there was always food on the table and always coal on the fire. We'd got plenty of fruit because my dad used to scythe the grass for the lady across the road and she'd got a huge orchard. She gave us lots of fruit: apples, pears, cherries. I remember when the coal was delivered, it was always dropped on the road. It was never put on the pavement, because they weren't allowed to. It was on the actual road, but there wasn't much traffic in those days. My dad would come home from the pit and have to start barrowing it round the back. That coal was useful because wages were so low.'

Roy Astle, who started work down the mine in 1954, remembers the free coal too, telling me, 'While I was at Granville pit we got concessionary coal. The delivery men used to chuck the lump coal on the road, and you'd have to get it in yourself. Before nationalisation, you had to work 20 years before you could get any concessionary coal when you retired. You used to have to pay to have it delivered. Smokeless coal was delivered free, but nobody had smokeless, so we had to pay. I can't remember what it cost, not a lot. It was only for the delivery, it wasn't for the coal. That was free, part of your wages. A lot of men would have packed up work down the pit if it hadn't been for that, and I think I would as well. I'm one of the few round here that still has it delivered.'

While a glimpse of a coalman delivering sacks of coal has disappeared in much of the country, in the former coalfield areas this nostalgic sight can still be seen!

Betty told me, 'I can never remember having new clothes except a dress at Sunday school anniversary time. My mother had paid a woman so much a week for me and my sister to get those new anniversary clothes. I never remember having new shoes, or going to a shop for shoes. We used to get secondhand shoes and clothes from stalls on the market. I can even remember having to wear clogs to go to school. I was very, very embarrassed, but we'd got to go to school and we'd got no shoes. I was ten or eleven, so it would have been just before 1950. I think there must have been

*Lee Harper delivering concessionary coal to an ex-miner
in Donisthorpe in 2006.*

other children there wearing them but I was embarrassed. Clogs were looked down on. We weren't many yards from school, but those clogs did clatter.'

Betty's education, like that of so many working class children in the 1940s and 1950s, was affected by lack of money. The uniform and books necessary for a grammar school entrant were simply too expensive for many parents to afford and scholarships were few. 'In those days you only sat the eleven-plus if your parents wanted you to, and I wasn't allowed to because of the cost of the uniform, though I was always in the top range of children in the exams. I was clever and everything came easy to me, and the day I found out what the library was, it was wonderful. I think they must have got fed up with me. I used to come home from Bolsover library with four books at a time, and a couple of days later I was back because I'd read them all. I used to read in bed by candlelight because there was no electricity in our bedrooms, just downstairs. My mum would get cross because I'd never got a full candle in my room. I'd used it up reading. That's how she knew what I'd been up to!'

Paul Liversuch, who left school in 1963 and went straight into mining, was brought up from an early age by his grandmother. 'I lived with my grandma from the age of about eight or nine, because of problems at home. So I was brought up in an area in Castle Gresley where it was all miners. We could hear the pits at Cadley Hill from where we lived. You could set your clock by the pit winding gear. I'd see the night shift coming out, and I would talk to the miners as they came off shift, but I never thought I would work down it myself.

'My grandma played a major role in my life. Her father had experienced poverty and hardship, and therefore it was bred into you. You were taught as a child about the miners' struggles. It wasn't just a case of "Oh, we had a strike in such and such a year", you were taught what it was all about. My grandma was very adamant about the NUM [National Union of Mineworkers], though my dad, who was not a miner, was very anti. Grandma instilled into me from an early age that it was important to join the union. I used to have a history lesson on all the struggles and strikes that had taken place in the past, and how the union had improved the miners' working conditions.

'I remember one particular day when there was a knock at the door and it was Coal Board officials. And they said to her, "Can

Gresley pit in the early 1900s, showing how close some pits were to where the miners lived. (SDMPG)

you come with us?" A friend of hers had died, been killed in Cadley Hill colliery, and they asked my grandmother if she could go and help break the news, because they didn't feel they could do it. It was that sort of experience that influenced me. You'd see adversity, you'd see struggle and you'd see all sorts of things that you'd never get in a normal job. It taught me so much.

'I remember another incident during the 1972 strike. My grandma used to tell me to come over to her home – she was living in a pensioner's flat by then – and she'd give us food and different things. One day I was coming out of her flat, and a lady from up the road turned to my grandmother and says, "Well, Mrs Liversuch, I think it's about time the miners accepted the government offer and went back, don't you?" Now, Grandma was a very placid person, but that day she hit the roof. "Go back? How dare you say go back! They went back in 1926, but they're not going back now." She gave this woman a lecture in political history!'

Chapter 2

'Going Into Another World'

What was it like to go suddenly, often at the age of 15, from the child's world of school to a life among the men underground? Although many of the men to whom I spoke came from mining families where mining talk would be common, the transition from childhood to the life of a young miner must have been a shock to some.

Paul Liversuch trained at Donisthorpe pit in the 1960s, then spent three years at Cadley Hill, followed by 27 years back at Donisthorpe. He described with great clarity how he felt on his first day down the mine.

'In the training room it'd all be explained to you, but it was a bit like looking forward to having a tooth out, you knew the day would come, the first time you'd got to go down the pit. The first experience of going down the shaft – especially at Donisthorpe where the shaft had got a bend in it so the cages shook as they crossed – was very frightening. The older men would be smiling, because they knew that when there was someone in the cage on his first time down, the engine winder would lay it a bit fast. I suppose it was to get you immune to it.

The shaft rising from the pit bottom at Clay Cross No 2 pit.
The age of the boy on the right indicates that the photograph
was taken before 1911, when the age for underground work
was raised to 14, and later to 15. (Cliff Williams)

'When you got to the pit bottom, you wondered what to expect, because you didn't have a clue, no matter what you'd been told about it. It was a surprise to see everything at the pit bottom painted white. Then you'd go to a training face, an old seam that wasn't working and they showed you all the different ways and methods of support. Eventually you went onto a real face and seeing a solid wall of coal, completely black, was awe-inspiring. Nothing prepares you for it, if you know what I mean. You had to learn just what it was like to turn your light out. You never knew what darkness was till you turned your light out. It was complete black.

'It literally is going into another world, where everything's different. It's like being a child again. You have to learn to do things from the very start. The main thing you have to learn is to

The shaft cage at Pilsley pit. (Cliff Williams)

look after yourself, so you know how to put your equipment on. It's almost like road safety. You have to learn the dangers of walking up a road where haulage trucks might be going up and down. You have to learn about conveyor belts coming down, and there'd be junctions leading to another road. And at Donisthorpe you'd have to learn about smells, because in one direction you'd have an intake of fresh air and then you'd have a return where the air smelt musty going out.

'From the bottom of the shaft you went on a manrider, or to some faces you'd have to walk. We had one face about four miles out and we'd come out on a conveyor, but to most faces we walked. We walked probably two miles and part of that you would be bent double, you couldn't stand up. The roadway was meant to be 14 ft high, but for about a mile you'd be walking with your back bent. You couldn't straighten up because there wasn't room to straighten up. I don't think my back's ever recovered, to be honest.'

A man-rider in Holmewood pit, which would transport miners from the shaft to the coalface. (John Burrows)

When I asked Roy Astle about his first time going down the shaft at Granville pit in 1954, he told me, 'God, that was a shock. It was steam winding, yes, steam winding, and down a big shaft. When the cage was loaded with men, they'd ring off, then they used to drop you fast. It was faster than electric, much faster than electric. The shaft at Shonky, on the site where the ski slope in Swadlincote is now, that was the deepest shaft in this area. That went down to the face they called Raker. But there they'd only got two guide ropes, and the cages used to touch the sides at times. It went that slow it took a good five minutes to come up, and it would catch the brickwork.

Another man who recalls his trip down in the cage is John Wileman from South Derbyshire, who put his thoughts into a poem:

The Cage

13 men in the cage
Gabbling about sport, politics, sex,
About what they did last night,
What they're going to do in the future,
What's going to happen to the industry.

13 men with snap-tins and water bottles
Going to their picnic underground –
Cheese sandwiches,
Meat sandwiches,
Salad sandwiches,
Coal-dust sandwiches.

13 men breathing the same air –
At the top it's fresh,
At the bottom it's cold and damp.
Breathing doesn't come easy underground,
Underground is a different life,
Underground you might feel like striking a man.

13 men in the cage,
Rubbing shoulders together,
Arguments forgotten,
Fathers and sons, all mates together.
The first thing we do on the surface
Is head for water.

Walter Burrows' first day at the pit was very different because he didn't actually get to do any work. He explained, 'I'll tell you about my first day at Markham. When I'd done all my basic training to work underground, I went to Markham on my first shift as an actual workman. My dad and brothers went down to their end of the colliery, and all the workmen were stood in a heap. A chap called Tom Swain, who was the NUM secretary, later MP for North East Derbyshire, he was shouting, and eventually he asked all of us did we want to go to work or did we want to go home? Everybody put their hands up to go back home, including me because I followed the rest. And I was on strike. I had to get changed again and go home and knocked my mother up, and she said, "What's this all about?" I said, "I don't know what it means but I'm on strike." That was my first day as a miner, but we did go back to work the next day.

Walter had not wanted to be a miner at all but had to face the hard economic reality of life in a mining family. 'I started work in 1950. I wanted to join the RAF actually – I'd been in the Air Training Corps for three years – but I couldn't join the RAF until I was 17 years old. I was 15 so I went down the pit for two years. When I was 17, I went and sat four examinations for acceptance into the RAF, at Cranwell College. I came home on my first leave and obviously I could see we were struggling. There were a lot of kids at home, and my dad had had an accident and was on low pay. So I went back to college and said, "Look I'm going to have to finish, I'm needed at home more than I'm needed here." So I went back down the pit.

'I did all work underground as a haulage worker till I was 18 years old, when I became a coalface worker, a development

An early 20th-century view of Granville colliery, with No 1 shaft and screens in the foreground and No 2 shaft in the background. (SDMPG)

worker, and then when I was 23, a shot firer. That's when I joined NACODS, the National Association of Colliery Overmen, Deputies and Shotfirers, and when I was 25, I became a deputy. A deputy is the name for the man deputising for the colliery manager.'

Walter's younger brother, John, explained the family background: 'I was one of eleven kids, six lads, five lasses. Only one of the lads didn't ultimately work in the pits, and he worked on the railways. Even some of the lasses worked at the pits. For three or four generations we were coal miners, and I'm proud of that. Mum married my dad after the First World War, after her first husband got killed in the war. We had a fairly standard bringing up, poor mining background, no money and plenty of love. Always a bit of snap on the table, perhaps not always the best sort, lard and salt, that sort of thing.

'I went to school at Duckmanton Infants School, which had been bombed during the war, so my first school days were spent in the temporary schoolroom in the chapel. I were that bad at going to school as a five-year-old that they used to have to fetch my brother out of top class to look after me. Well, my dad died on my thirteenth birthday. I came home from school, full of life on my thirteenth birthday, and my dad had died.

'I didn't pass the eleven-plus, unlike our Walt who did. It went like that in our family: eldest lad passed, next 'un didn't, next eldest lad did, next 'un didn't, next 'un did and I didn't. I started work at Markham pit at 15, as everybody did, and I hated the place. I were put in a pit bottom job, simply watching the tubs coming off the chair up two separate levels. My job was to stop 'em meeting on the point where they came together. Bored, dreadful, lonely, dark – I hated it. I stuck it for a while but kept coming home poorly.

'It got to the point where obviously the powers-that-be spoke to my eldest brother Ellis, who at that time was a deputy. Ultimately he said to me, "Why dun't tha go for a mechanical apprenticeship?" So I said, "Good idea, I will", because I was always into that sort of thing. I applied, got an interview, got accepted, went onto an apprenticeship, and transferred to Ireland colliery as a consequence.

'It was the best move I ever made, because while I was at Markham, I'd got so many members of the family there – brothers, uncles – I was never John Burrows. I was always "Ellis's brother" or "Walt's brother", or somebody's nephew. I went down Ireland pit as an apprentice fitter. First day there, I got changed, and I had to clock on – I'd never had to clock on before, I'd always had a check. This was 1957, a year after I'd started at Markham, and it was the best move I ever made. I enjoyed every minute.'

When I asked John how he felt on going down the shaft for the first time, his reply was very different from those of Paul Liversuch and Roy Astle. John answered, 'Going down the shaft never bothered me, it wasn't a consideration. I'd already been to Grassmoor Training, so I was aware of the process. The only time anybody ever bothered about it was after the shaft disaster at Markham, but even that didn't deter 99% of people. It was a freak one-off incident, and I'm always preaching – I always have preached – that riding the shaft was the safest ride in the world. When you think about it, the number of times the shaft has been ridden and the number of men, and look at the number of incidents that happened in the shaft, it's still the safest journey you'll ever take.

'Let me tell you what happened at home on my first day. When I got up, my mother got up with me, as she had done with all the lads – packed my snap, made me a cup of tea, never stopped talking. Five o'clock in the morning, and she never stopped talking, totally unusual for my mother. The others had gone 'cos they'd got to get there earlier than me. I got home from work that day, got asked how I'd got on, said okay, that were end of conversation. And I said to my mother, "Don't get up with me any more. I don't want a woman talking and yattering at five o'clock in the morning." And she said, "Thank you very much. That's what everybody else said to me." She'd purposely got up that morning to talk and talk and talk so I would say, "Don't get up." She was very, very clever. And she didn't get up any more, and I didn't want her to.'

Terry Butkeraitis grew up in the mining village of Whitwell, though he didn't work at the pit there to begin with. Terry himself is Derbyshire-born and bred, but his unusual surname comes from his father, a Lithuanian, who came to work in the Derbyshire pits after the 1939-45 war. When Terry was 15 he left school, and his last day was quite eventful. "I was in a Catholic school. I weren't due to leave school till the summer of 1965, but before Easter I'd applied for a job with the Coal Board, the NCB as it was then, and I'd got interviewed and did some tests and exams and actually got a job as an apprentice electrician. I'll never forget the school headmaster sending for me this day. They were staunch Roman Catholics, and I'd got to have a thrashing for smoking in the toilets. So I got my six-of-the-best in front of the school at lunchtime when we had assembly, then in the afternoon he sent for me and said you can leave school early because you've got a job.

33

Oakthorpe Steps in 1977. (SDMPG)

The canteen at Measham pit in the early 1970s. (SDMPG)

'I grew two foot taller that week because I were going to work. But one thing I learned: school had never, ever prepared me for work. It was such a shock, a culture shock, to go and strip off in a bath with your uncles, with people you'd looked on as grown men and you were still a child. It was a bit of an embarrassment to step into a communal shower and scrub yoursen'. It were a bit daunting and frightening. I'll never forget that.

'I started at Oxcroft pit, which was a drift mine. And my first day at the pit I went along and I was put with an old Communist. He still wore a flat cap and his helmet on top. He was the union secretary. In them days the union used to put a tin down to collect the subs, and I joined the union, the NUM. I worked at Oxcroft all through my apprenticeship, then I moved to Manton pit just a mile over the border into South Yorkshire.

'From the very first day of getting there, it was like dropping off the end of the earth and going to hell. It was the deepest mine

Not every miner was as well protected as this advertisement suggests – but the knee pads were still essential at Manton!

shaft in Europe. I'd come from a pit where you wore a donkey jacket and overalls. Everybody at Manton were looking at me as I was going down for the first time. I didn't realise till I got to the bottom that all they wore were their boots, their kneepads, and a pair of women's tights with the legs cut out, to stop their danglers thrashing about. It was very hot and dangerous. It took me two years to get away from there, because in them days they wouldn't let you just transfer from pit to pit. It were seen as poaching men. Anyway, nobody wanted jobs in pits in those days because a bus driver and a farm worker were getting more money.

'I then moved to Whitwell pit, back in North Derbyshire, which was similar to Oxcroft except it were a shaft mine. Whitwell were a nice family pit, you knew everybody. Because Whitwell had got every type of conditions that you could ever encounter in a mine – wet, cold, hot, dusty, inclines, broken strata – they used it as an experimental pit for trying out all new machinery. If it worked at Whitwell, it would work anywhere else, so we were at the forefront of new technology. It was a happy pit. It were one where the management and the unions shared the responsibility and the management were pretty fair, at least until the strike.'

Ron Wain started at Stanton Lane, also known as Bretby No 3, after three weeks' training at Donisthorpe. He later worked at Bretby Drift and Donisthorpe collieries, ending up as a deputy. He remembers the pit ponies that were still used in a number of pits when he started work: 'I hated being a pony lad. They'd got one, Nova, and he were wild. The biggest pony they'd got. I had to turn him round against the face, and one place was only 10 ft by 8 ft, another was 8 ft by 8 ft. Well, you ain't got a lot of room, especially if there was subsidence!'

One man who would disagree about working with ponies was Roy Astle, who told me, 'We had ponies at both pits at Granville, the Big Pit and the Little Pit. When Donisthorpe went over to haulages and did away with their ponies, they were sent to Granville. I'm very near sure that Granville was the last pit round this area to have ponies down the pit. I enjoyed working with them.'

*Ponies were still being used underground in the second half of the
20th century, though not all were as friendly as this picture suggests!
(Magic Attic Archives)*

Chapter 3

'Not Just A Job'

When asked the question, 'What was the best thing about working down the pit?', virtually everyone I spoke to came up with the same answer – 'The comradeship'. Asked to elaborate, they told me that because miners relied on each other for their safety, it built up a sense of solidarity that went beyond friendship. A miner would stand by his fellow-colliers, whether it was over a work problem or in a dispute with the management.

Paul Liversuch, who worked mainly at Donisthorpe colliery in the South Derbyshire coalfield, explained: 'Working in the pits, you see, if somebody was behind with the job or having some difficulty, and you'd finished your job, you were expected to go and give a hand. I say it was expected, but it was automatic, you just did it. When somebody was in trouble you'd give them a hand. Everything was built round the fact that you'd got to rely on each other. There was never an isolated incident that was nothing to do with you. For instance, if there was a dispute on one face, it affected all of us. So you stuck together, you had to. I mean, say, even if it looked like nothing to do with us, that didn't

A group of comrades at Cadley Hill in 1984. (SDMPG)

matter. It *was* something to do with us. The idea was, if it wasn't sorted out, we could be doing the same thing tomorrow and then it *would* affect us. And so you learned solidarity. As I always say, coal mining was not just a job, it was a way of life.'

John Burrows, of Ireland pit in the north-east of the county, gave a perfect example of how a miner could get involved in a problem that superficially had nothing to do with his own work. He told me, 'Throughout my apprenticeship, for whatever reason – I suppose because I was a bit gobby – the rest of the lads used to turn to me when there was any sort of trouble, and I used to stand up to the gaffers. I was warned for it many, many times, which only made me more determined. I was young and stroppy, and hefty enough to look after missen' – because you'd got to be physically hefty in the sort of work I did.

'And at 19 what really set me on the path to trade union activities was connected to one of the surface fellows out of the stockyard who had been working with me in the week. He had a bit of a grumble about how he had to come and do all this work in the week to set things up, but at weekends the surface men never got any overtime. He said, "I've got to go to buy stuff at the same shop as you, and my kids have got to eat the same sort of food as yours." And I thought, Crikey, he's right.

'So, I went to the surface engineers and said, "Why can't Jack and a couple of his mates come and work the weekend, because we're always struggling for staff?" "What's that got to do with you?" they said. I explained, "Well he's been working Wednesday through to Friday preparing the job with me, doing probably a bit more work than me towards getting it ready, and I've got to come in at the weekend but he can't." I didn't want to come in every Saturday and Sunday anyway but as an apprentice fitter it was

A miner at work at Measham in 1970. (SDMPG)

required of you. I was an apprentice craftsman and he were a surface labourer, and there weren't ever any work for surface labourers at the weekend.

'And I said, "Well, I'll tell you what, if some of them can't start to have a weekend shift, I don't want to work every Saturday and Sunday." Their response was, "Don't you start talking like that. As a fitter, you'll be expected to work whenever we want you to work." It wasn't a question of Can-I-have-some-overtime? It was a question of Can-I-have-a day-off? And it all got a bit heated, and some of the other lads said, "Well, let's all stop then. We'll none of us come in this weekend." On Friday afternoon, the engineer, the big mester, sent for me with the intention of giving me a dressing down, and when I went in, he said, "What's all this that you're on about, setting all these men up to work and I don't want them to work?" I said, "Well, you don't have to, but if they don't get a shift or the promise of a shift in the future, I'm not coming in tomorrow. I don't know about the others, but I'm not coming in. So, that's it. I'll go home now then." So the balloon went up. I went home that afternoon, on strike.

'The fitters were in a dilemma, 'cos if one person went home, everyone else went home. It happened like that in them days. The fitters went home, so no fitters, no maintenance, no shaft examination. It was never my intention for it to spread. The night shift colliers got to know. They got the word that I'd gone home because I was standing up for the surface stockyard men, and they said, "Well, if he's big enough to do that and lose his money, we're big enough to help him." So the night shift went home. And of course the next day, there was no work done, no Saturday and Sunday work done, no maintenance done.

'The result was that on Monday morning the whole job were going to stop. On the Sunday, the manager sent the union secretary for me and for a couple of fitters and for the craftsmen's rep, to try and get it sorted out, so that they could get started on Monday. Remember I were only a kid, and there was all these big mesters round me, so I said, "Look, I didn't want any of this. All I wanted was to get these blokes who were

A miner operating the catchpoints on the underground railway at Measham (top) and driver Malcolm Heath at Shirebrook colliery. High speed transport could be dangerous underground and miners had to look out for each other. (SDMPG)

doing all this preparation work a Saturday shift or a Sunday shift." The manager asked, "Well why can't they have one? After all, they've got to use the same shops as the rest of us." "That's exactly what we said," I told him, "they've got to go to the same shop." That struck a chord with the manager, and he said, "We'll put it right. It'll be put right next weekend. Now, can I get the men to work today and get this shaft examined?" I said, "You can for me, boss." I couldn't believe it. We'd got what we wanted, more than we wanted, actually. So, to cut a long story short, we sorted that out.

'I thought that the then craftsmen's rep were starting to be a bit bigoted, so I said, "I'm not having a rep that's got no backbone representing me," and while I was only 19, I decided I would stand as the craftsmen's rep. When I stood and got elected, I was the youngest NUM branch committee man in the county definitely, probably in the country.'

A sense of fair play had started John on a path of trade union activism. Four years later he was elected as the branch delegate, representing not just the craftsmen, but the coalface workers and surface workers as well. It was unusual for someone from the craft side of the Union to be elected by the whole workforce, but John had proved his solidarity with them.

The feeling of comradeship was evident during the year-long strike in 1984-85. Terry Butkeraitis told me, 'I was the branch president at Whitwell pit, so I had a little bit more responsibility. I looked round the surrounding areas and we'd got Cresswell pit, which was in Derbyshire but always counted as a Nottinghamshire pit, and so the strikers there were getting nothing because the UDM [Union of Democratic Mineworkers] had took over in Nottinghamshire and sequestrated all the funds. So we had to take on board all the Cresswell miners who were on strike, to pay them out-of-pocket expenses.'

Terry told me with pride how the village of Whitwell was organised during the strike, even finding tasks for those men who had been banned by the courts from going on the picket lines. 'We ran a full socialist economy in Whitwell village. We had miners that were took off picket lines for actions that they were later found not guilty of, they were sawing logs, for example. And everybody had a bag of logs every week, including all the pensioners. There was a local wood that we'd got permission to go and get logs from. We had a group that couldn't go on picket lines because of their bail conditions, so we had them delivering food parcels.

'That 1984 Christmas were a bit unique for us in our village. We were adopted by some trade unionists in London, and it's over 20 years on since the strike and they still rank among my best friends. I still see them 20 or 30 times a year in the work that I do now, and that friendship has gone on all that time. These people raised thousands and thousands of pounds and I'll never forget that in winter weather they biked all the way to Whitwell village from the Houses of Parliament. It took them three days and they raised £13,000.

'And this is when we learned who in the local community were supportive of us. It was Christmas time, and I had to order 850 chickens, 850 little bags of 'taters, 850 tins of ham, a full Christmas dinner and a pudding for every miner's family that were on strike in our pit and at Cresswell as well. So this were a huge order, 850 chickens, 850 bags of sprouts, 850 pieces of pork, all the trimmings you'd have with your Christmas dinner. So I went to Morrisons, Tesco, Asda and all these places. I think we finally agreed with Tesco – and Tesco was a cheap man's supermarket then, and not the rich shop it is today. And they actually supplied us. It was literally a 40-ft trailer lorry that they brought the food on.

'We were making all these bags up, and then these cyclists rode into the village and they saw the food parcels being given out, and the toys and everything. And they actually helped in giving them out to the families. So Christmas brought a great deal of satisfaction for me that we'd actually provided that, through trade unionists and people that supported us. The cyclists were London businessmen, solicitors, GLC workers, all sorts of sympathisers.

'I've got three children – they'd be three, six and nine at that time – and the kids were quite reconciled to have nothing for Christmas, because we were on strike, we'd no money, we were in debt. I didn't remember this until my son was being interviewed about two years ago for a magazine about the strike. I read this article in the paper, they were asking him what he recollected of the strike, and he said, "I remember at Christmas, I were expecting no toys, we didn't know whether we were going to get a Christmas dinner and what it were going to be." He said, "I went and smashed open my piggy bank and I give my dad £50 to buy presents with." I'd forgot all about that until I read this article last year. To give it him back now it'd probably be worth £5,000 with interest!

'But that Christmas, because the kids didn't expect a lot, was probably the best Christmas we've ever had. If you look at the

Some of the cyclists who arrived in Whitwell in December 1984 on the sponsored bike ride from the House of Commons in London, in support of the striking miners. (Terry Butkeraitis)

Christmas of today where they've got computers, and they expect the world, in them days they didn't expect anything but they got something. It was probably the least pressurized and stress-free Christmas we'd ever had.'

Although John Burrow's brother, Walter, was a deputy at Markham colliery, and therefore part of the management, he summed up the feeling of the mining community about the solidarity of the pit. Walter told me, 'The comradeship underground was – and it had got to be – all for one and one for all, because if anybody made a mistake it could have been a disaster for other people. We all had to work for each other, in everything we did.'

Chapter 4

Three Foot Seams and Desperate Mice

Ex-miners recall vividly the varying conditions in the pits where they worked and the problems they faced with dust or water, with heat or cold, and working in cramped positions.

Walter Burrows explained, 'At Markham we worked the Outcoal seam that was only 2 ft thick, north of the Deepsoft seam that was 7 ft 6 ins thick. So we'd got people working on their knees on the 2-ft seam, and we'd got other people working where they could actually put their hands above their head and still not reach the roof.'

Paul Liversuch, who worked in South Derbyshire, described the conditions in more detail. 'You'd have seams such as the ones we called Littlewood Field and Raker and Woodford – they were all small seams. You'd have Main Coal that was 6 ft high, and Stockinger, that was a high seam. So it varied, it was never all the same. You had to get used to working in cramped conditions. The majority of my pit life was working on seams that were 3 ft or 3 ft 6 ins high, and so you had to learn to work in very low conditions, on your knees. At the end of a shift, it was a real joy to stand up. It was like walking on air when you finished at the coal face. You can't experience anything like it. You take it for granted you can walk, but once you come away from working at a low face you can straighten your back. Also you can pull your trousers up, because half the time they'd be halfway down your backside and you hadn't had room to pull them up. You'd got pieces of coal stuck between your kneepads and down your trousers. You were knocking your back on supports, and your back would be sore for the first few days.

'There was a job called ripping, where you were drilling stone all day long, and some weeks instead of being 10 ft high it'd come down to 7 ft high. You had to learn to lift heavy girders, you had to know where to put your holes or otherwise you'd fire too much or fire too little and it'd cause you a lot of work. You had to know how much power to use to blow them down. Ripping was a very, very skilled job – and you did it at the edge of the face. I was a ripper but I also worked on coalface timbering when it caved in a lot. That was another skilled job and a very dangerous job. And heading, where you drive a new roadway out, or a face out, I did some of that. That was very hard, difficult work.

'You had to drill for the coal or sometimes you had machinery that cut out the new road. When I first went, it was all a matter of drilling, and firing it down, and the coal going to a conveyor. Sometimes you had to shovel it out, literally, all day. Eventually you had things like joyloaders that filled it out, and machines as the Eimco, a mechanical shovel on rails that would tip it onto the conveyors. In other words you had mechanical loading, but when I first went in, it was all by hand and it was very, very hard work.

'You worked in extremes. You'd go from extreme cold where you'd have to wear a donkey jacket, to conditions of extreme heat where you'd just wear a vest and sweat would be pouring down

*A pony pulls a train of full tubs from the coalface to the pit bottom,
a task later taken over by conveyors. (Cliff Williams)*

your back. It would be so hot that it was an effort just to walk.
And you worked in conditions where there was so much dust you
could just see a fog. Other times there was water pouring on you,
and you'd have to come out early.'

Austin Fairest is another collier who worked in a wet pit, and
he recalls with wry amusement the trouble he had with one
manager who was reluctant to admit the problem. 'In one pit,
High Moor, the main problem was wetness. Water dripped in
constantly from the roof. The miners in wet pits could get
concessions because of the terrible conditions – more pay, and the
right to finish earlier so they could change out of wet clothes
before going home.' One manager was reluctant to grant the
concessions, and Austin asked him to take a look at the excess
water. Austin walked him through a swiller, an underground
puddle, 400 yards long and 4 feet deep. 'I was dressed for the job,
but the manager was in ordinary boots. For part of the way we

even had to walk along a conveyer belt. When we eventually got to the end, the manager glared round truculently, and said, "Where's this bloody water, then?"

Other difficult situations included the danger of fire and gas, and problems with the roof caving in. Paul Liversuch told me, 'We had a lot of problems with Main Coal seam because it tended to fire when it got too warm, so it'd have to be sealed off. You'd have problems with gas with different seams. At Main Coal you'd have methane gas, and other places you'd have gas called "black damp" where it'd come from the floor upwards. There was never one day the same. There was always something different.

'You'd have problems with keeping the roof in. We used wooden props in certain areas because sometimes you couldn't take a machine through so you'd revert to the old method. It was a very dangerous job, timbering a roof when it had fallen in, but

---

A deputy at Clay Cross No 2 pit testing for methane gas,
an ever present danger throughout the mining era. (Cliff Williams)

you'd got to know what to do, or else you could kill yourself and kill other people. You couldn't just send anybody on that job, you had to send somebody who knew what they were doing, because there was a skill in doing it. I mean, the first thing you had to do when you had a fall, you had to strengthen the good ground that you'd got, so it didn't spread. But you had to look after yourself. You had to look for something to cover yourself, but you also had to watch if it started coming again and find somewhere to get out on the road quick. Sometimes the floor would heave up, so you'd have to what they call dent it, get it up. The weight of the rock would press down at the side and it'd push the middle up. You could have a seam – it might sound silly – 6 ft high, yet the roadways up to it might be about 3 ft where the floor had come up. Sometimes the trucks would come off the road and you had to learn how to get them on again, because you hadn't got lifting gear. You had to know how to prise them on again.'

Another old photograph showing two deputies making inspections at Clay Cross No 2 pit (note the stick – a badge of office). Technology may have advanced by the mid 20th century, but a roof fall still created dangerous conditions for all miners underground. (Cliff Williams)

Another problem was caused by the fact that the men ate their snap where they worked. They would leave their leftovers at the side of the roadway – and that attracted mice. Ron Harvey said, 'I'll tell you an incident that happened at Gresley. The men in the gate road used to have a big transformer and all the switchgear. And it was warm there because the transformer used to heat up. When the men came off the face at snap time (break time), they all congregated there because it was warm. All the bits of food were chucked down there. Well, the mice all came and the place was snived out with them. Now obviously the fitter and the electrician had to stand there and wait in case of a breakdown on the face. And we used to get fed up because you'd only got to sit down, and you'd got these mice all the way round you.

'But every couple of weeks as the face advanced, the electricians used to come, usually on a Friday night, and move the transformer, the switchgear, may be 50 yards. They used to come, usually on a Friday night, and move all the switchgear forward. Now for a week in the new place you never saw a mouse. Not one. But after a week, the mice used to have *their* move up, and they all came forward. They were all back again. We'd to say to the electricians, "Look, the mice are having their move up now."

'I've worked during the August shutdown, when all the miners went on their two-week summer holidays, and I was working on a machine where I'd got to lie full length to do the job. And as I lay there, my leg kept itching, scratching, and I suddenly realised a mouse had gone right up my overall leg. I just smacked it dead. Because during the shutdown, the mice had no food and by the end of the fortnight they used to get desperate, they'd eat one another. I think over later years they used to put poison down to kill them, but not in them days.'

Paul Liversuch had mentioned the change from working by hand to using machinery, and Walter Burrows informed me that many of the new machines were first trialled at a Derbyshire colliery. 'Because Markham was so huge and we'd got such different, varied circumstances, all the coal cutting machines that they'd invented and devised were sent to Markham to be tried out.

We made some of them work, but we trialled some that hadn't got a cat in hell's chance, that had faults and dropped to bits.

'The best ever was a shearing machine called the Huwood Shearer. That proved to be the most successful coal cutting machine in the world. It doesn't matter where in the world you go now, that machine in different forms is still being used. It was the most reliable and produced more coal than any other machine. We had some other good machines. The Dosco machine, which was Canadian, took 5 ft of coal out at once but, because it was only what's called a cyclic machine, you could only do one cut every 24 hours, so all the bywork had got to be done ready before it started again. With the Huwood Shearer machine, once we'd got to one end of the coalface, we could move about and start cutting back the other way. It didn't rely on other equipment being used, that's why you could cut forever with a Shearer machine.

'But eventually we proved that the mining equipment that British coal mining engineers had devised was still the best in the world. It didn't matter wherever you went in the world, you'd find the best coal cutting machinery was British.'

Chapter 5

Missing Fingers and the Kebab

Because of the rough conditions, and the nature of the job, many accidents occurred in coal mines. The more serious pit disasters, leading to multiple loss of life, are dealt with in the following chapter, but there were also accidents to individuals. Austin Fairest told me about a miner at Whitwell pit who had a nasty accident in the mid-1980s. He was unloading wooden dowels from a steel crawler belt, and it was important to pick them up carefully. The dowels were 8 ft long, with one end square and the main shaft round with a chamfered end. As he went to pick one dowel up, the belt forced it upwards through his body, and out the other side. To take him to hospital, the dowel had to be sawed off, back and front. Luckily it had missed all his vital organs, and the man recovered and went back to work. It wasn't long before he had a new nickname; following his accident he was always known as 'Kebab'.

Two miners at Measham demonstrating a rescue stretcher in the early 1970s.
(SDMPG)

Another man suffered an accident to his foot. He took off his boot and found it full of blood. He then removed his sock, only to find that three of his toes were still in it. His only comment was a phlegmatic, 'That looks a bugger.' The man was back having a drink in the pub the next day.

Although all are aware that collieries are inherently dangerous places, the occasional miner will act incautiously. It was known for men coming up in the cage to open the gate before reaching the top, so they could leap out as soon as possible. Austin even told me of one who used the cage during speed trials. At one pit with a 440 yard shaft, the winder managed 58 winds in an hour! The man who took a fast ride was extremely foolhardy, but did escape injury.

Not all incidents turned into accidents, fortunately. Ron Wain remembered one near-catastrophe that happened. 'On my first job as deputy we were firing rips down. I was ready to shout "Fire!" but I felt there was something wrong. No one seemed to be missing but I still felt I had to go and check again, so I went back to the face, and there was this chap, Big Jeff we called him, sitting in the dark, eating his snap. He was stone deaf, you see, caused by an injury playing rugby, and he hadn't heard what was going on. He had a near miss, that day.'

Paul Liversuch mentioned a serious incident that happened on the coalface at Donisthorpe in the early 1980s. 'We'd got somebody buried and we had to get him out with our bare hands, two of us did. It was a roof fall, and he was buried underneath. I locked the conveyer out, then crawled up it to get to him as quick as I could. You had to use quick thinking. The deputy was panicking at the time, and I told him he'd got to calm down. There was no need to get in a state, we were going to get the man out. We knew where he was and we'd got every intention of getting him out. It's hard to explain but there was an adrenaline pump. You knew you were in danger yourself, but your main concern was the danger of somebody else. And that's what pit life was about. You had to not only look after yourself but learn to look after other people, because you couldn't just leave anything.

You'd got the responsibility of caring for somebody else. The man was buried for about 20 minutes, but if it hadn't been for quick thinking and quick action by two or three of us, he would have been dead. We got him out just in time before the whole lot came down. Some time afterwards, he came to my house and saw my wife Christine and said, "I wouldn't be sitting here if it hadn't have been for Paul's quick thinking."

'Then I went to an incident where somebody had had their fingers ripped off, and we had to get him out. The haulage rope had stuck fast and he went to free it. I could see it happening and I shouted not to do it, but he was young lad and before I could stop him, the tension of it cut his fingers off. I was the only man on the scene so, of course, I had to take some action. I had to hold him up and also organise someone to come to give me a hand. A deputy came. We had to move him first to somewhere where it was warm. I did first aid on him, put his arm in a sling. We had to get him out as quickly as possible, he'd lost his fingers; well, two were hanging off. One he did eventually lose completely. He was losing blood and we didn't know the entire state he was in, and the only thing we could do was get him to the pit bottom as soon as possible and get professional help. And the only way we could get him out – he was in pain and semi-conscious, he was coming and going – was to put him on a stretcher and drag him through what we call a snigget, a little roadway about 4 ft high. We dragged him for about 1,000 yards, but that was the only way to get him to the shaft as quick as we possibly could. We got him up an incline of about one in six, manhandled him up there, because we daren't risk anything else. There was no conveyor, nothing we could transport him on.' When I asked Paul why it had fallen to him to do the first aid, he simply replied, 'Well, there was nobody else there at the time.'

Paul himself met with an accident at the end of his pit career. He had told me that he had worked for three years at Cadley, followed by 27 years at Donisthorpe. When I asked him whether he was at Donisthorpe when the pit shut in 1990, he told me, 'More or less, but I had an accident when I broke my cheekbone

Accidents did happen underground and most were dealt with by fellow miners, but permanent rescue staff were available if needed – this team from Chesterfield Rescue Station were being filmed for the NCB information film 'Fires Underground'. (John Burrows)

and my collarbone, so I finished a year early. I was still off sick when the pit closed.' I asked him what caused the accident and he explained, 'Something was buried in the coal and a machine disc hit it. It hit me in the face and I was quite poorly for six months.'

Paul concluded, 'You had the experience of seeing nasty accidents. You learned how to cope, and you saw things that were not very nice. When I worked at Cadley Hill there was a man got his head fast in a tension box. I didn't see it myself but I know someone who did and he never worked down the pit again because it so affected him. You saw things, you saw some bad accidents, and you learned how to handle things, because of the conditions and because of how you worked. It came automatically.'

Chapter 6

Pit Disasters

When a serious accident occurs in a colliery, the difficult conditions and the fact that hundreds of men are working deep underground can soon turn an incident into a major disaster. Derbyshire has had a number of such tragedies. One occurred at Markham pit in 1938, when 79 men died and a further 40 were injured. Another was at Cresswell in 1950, when 80 men died. And a third was again at Markham, in 1973, when 19 men were killed and 11 seriously injured.

On Monday, 10 May 1938 an underground explosion occurred at just after 5.30 am, half an hour before the end of the night shift. There were over 170 men working on the Blackshale seam, some 690 yards below ground. The seam had been worked since the mid-1920s and was ventilated by two shafts, the No 1 downcast and the No 4 upcast, although by 1938 all the coalface work was taking place some distance away from these two shafts.

By 5.30 am, most of the nightshift men who worked at the coalface – rippers, hauliers and shotfirers – were on their way to the pit bottom. Two minutes later, there was a noise 'like a heavy bump', and a cloud of dust 'like a blue wave' knocked them down.

Dealing with a pit fire: the Mines Rescue Service in a training exercise.
(John Burrows)

The ones nearest to it were knocked unconscious. The disaster had been caused by a coal dust explosion – there were many tubs of coal dust waiting to be taken to the pit bottom, then to the surface. Coal dust explosions are usually preceded by a firedamp explosion. However, on this occasion, no evidence of any firedamp was found and it was eventually concluded that some sparking or arcing must have ignited coal dust spilling from the tubs.

The first rescue team called out was from Chesterfield Rescue Station, soon followed by teams from Mansfield and Ilkeston. The Chesterfield men reached Markham at 6.25 am and were instructed to go to the stables – ponies were used in mines at that time – in the North Plane return. There Dr McKay treated a number of men, and then the rescuers proceeded further into the mine where they treated 35 men suffering from carbon monoxide poisoning, before handing them over to stretcher-bearers. At 7.30 am, the East Plane was entered, and a badly burned man was treated, and bodies of men were found along with a dead pony among damaged tubs and roof girders. Two fires, one in an engine house and a second by a wheel hole, were dealt with. More bodies were discovered, three alongside some derailed tubs and a fourth by the coalface. The Chesterfield rescue team were sent back to the surface at 8.40 am and the search was taken over by the Ilkeston and Mansfield men, who found more fires, dense smoke and more bodies. The rescue work continued until 10 pm on

A member of the Safety in Mines Research Establishment at Harpur Hill, near Buxton. (John Burrows)

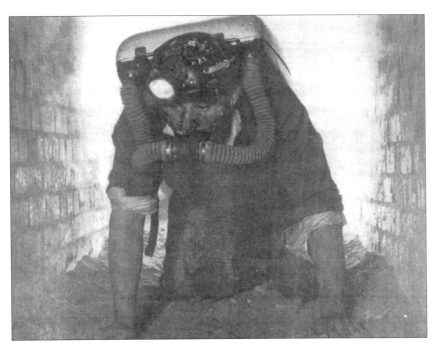

Wednesday, 12 May, some 65 hours after the explosion, with teams from Staveley, Langwith, Warsop, Markham and Ireland collieries having taken part.

In the 1938 Markham pit explosion, 79 colliers were killed and a further 40 were injured. All had the cause of death recorded as carbon monoxide poisoning, with some having 'violence and burns' as contributing factors. The fatalities ranged in age from an 18-year-old pony driver, Arthur Brown, to a 63-year-old shot firer, Herbert Brough. The list of the dead reveals the tragic fact that many were members of the same families, some being brothers and others father and son. Some of the women of north-east Derbyshire had lost both a husband and a son. The whole community mourned. It would be a good thing if the editors of those tabloid newspapers, that were to so disparage miners and mining communities during later times of strikes, were to read the list of the men who died in accidents like these.

A similar number of colliers, 80 in total, met their deaths in the fire that broke out at Cresswell pit in the early hours of Tuesday, 26 September 1950. Had the day shift been at work there would have been over 400 men working underground, but the night shift numbered 211. Friction was the original cause of the fire, which broke out on the main conveyer.

Henry Richardson, who worked at Cresswell for 32 years – he started there in 1950, a week after the disaster – explained to me that the day shift had noticed that the No 2 trunk belt was badly scored, with a groove in it about 6 inches from the edge and running for about 300 yards. It was still functioning, however, and a full shift of coal had been carried without any mishaps. It was left for the night shift to repair the damaged belt. However, the overman in charge of the night shift discovered that a length of coal on one face had not been filled off, and gave instructions that the belt should continue running until the coal was cleared. At 11 pm, the transfer point attendant noticed that the scoring had developed into a split, which he could put his hand through. In spite of this it was decided to continue running the belt, and it was not until 3.10 am that it was observed that the belt now had

The memorial to the victims of the 1950 Cresswell pit disaster.

65

a trailing end. Further investigation showed that the transfer hopper was full of torn belting and was on fire. It was now 3.45 am. Two portable fire extinguishers were tried; one failed to function and the other had little effect.

The Chesterfield Rescue Station received the call at 4.15 am, and recorded the emergency as an underground fire at the conveyer transfer point. Significantly, in the section marked 'Number of lives in danger', the official has put a dash. Obviously, the full danger was still not being recognised. When the undermanager arrived at the scene, he found that firefighters called in from other parts of the mine had connected fire hoses to the water main but had got no pressure, resulting in an ineffective trickle of water. More portable fire extinguishers were brought in and, together with sand to smother the fire, these seemed to have damped it down. A message was sent to the surface that the fire was nearly out. This was incorrect. The smoke and steam had hidden the fact that the fire had spread along the roadway. It quickly spread to the roof supports and pit props, and then engulfed the machinery, leaving men trapped behind a wall of flame. There were 99 men working in the area, and of these only 19 managed to get out alive.

Rescue workers brought out three bodies before the conditions meant that the area where the fire was raging had to be sealed off. No one could be alive behind the fire, and sealing off was the only way of extinguishing it and preventing it from spreading. This decision, made by colliery officials, the inspectorate and NUM representatives, meant that the remaining bodies had to be left where they lay, inside the sealed-off area. It is heartbreaking to note that one man helping to build the walls knew that his own father was one of those inside.

Twelve hours later the seals were opened and a further 44 bodies were bought out, but the following day it was announced that the fire was more extensive than had been thought and the area was resealed. It was almost a year before the seals were finally removed and the remaining bodies recovered.

The majority of the 80 dead came from the village of Cresswell.

NATIONAL COAL BOARD - EAST MIDLANDS DIVISION

CENTRAL RESCUE STATIONS

EMERGENCY CALLS FROM COLLIERIES

Name of Colliery _Cresswell_   Tel. No. **223 x208**

Nature of Occurrence :—

  Underground : (1) Explosion in _Underground Fire_ District.

    Approximate number of lives in danger ___ _High Hazel Seam_

    (2) Fire in _Trunk Conveyor Transfer Point_ District.

    Number of lives in danger

  Surface :—   Fire involving the

       _i.e._ the particular building on fire, such as screens, winding engine
       house, lamp cabin, etc.

       Lives in danger

  Winder Service :— (Mansfield only)

  Particulars of occurrence and of requirements : (Lives in danger   )

  Vehicle required to turn-out
  (Rescue Car, Fire Engine or Winder)

  Name of Colliery Manager/Official giving the call _Mr Palmer_

  Time of Call _4.15 am._ a.m.   Date _26.9.50_
                 p.m.

REPEAT MESSAGE TO SENDER

N.B. – Other station instructed to Turn-out _Mansfield_ Time _4.20_ a.m.
                      Stand-by   p.m.

(Signed) _Mr Ford_   Duty Man.

ANY FURTHER PARTICULARS OR MESSAGE OF SPECIAL IMPORTANCE

CRESWELL – SEPT. 1950

* ORIGINAL EMERGENCY CALL TO STATION *

Chesterfield Rescue Station's log of the emergency call out at Cresswell pit.

Just as in other pit disasters, some families lost more than one member. The Dodds family from Cresswell lost three brothers – John, Leslie and Ernest. A fourth brother, Joe, was on holiday or he would have been working in the area too. In a memorial garden within the village cemetery in Skinner Lane, a black marble memorial stone lists the names and ages of the dead.

Henry Richardson started work at Cresswell pit as a surveyor's assistant – they liked to tell people they were Assistant Surveyors, a much grander sounding title. They were generally known as *line lads*, because they had to paint white lines at the coal face 'so everybody kept straight'. Henry sometimes had to work where the sealed-in bodies had lain for nearly a year. Despite the fact that the area had undergone complete air changes and deep cleansing, he could always recognise the exact positions by the smell, which he described as vile. Henry also told me that the very last man to get out of the pit alive in the 1950 fire was a man named Jack Turner. In a sad twist of fate, when Jack was 80, he and his wife Marjorie both died in a fire at a Littlewoods store in Chesterfield on 7 May 1993.

In 1994, a group of teenagers from St Augustine's Youth Club in Chesterfield interviewed a number of miners and people connected with miners. Their interviews were later collected in a book called *Pitful of Memories*. Kelli Walker chose to interview the Rev Stanley Branson, who had been the vicar of Cresswell at the time of the 1950 tragedy. He told her, 'It shook the whole place; Cresswell was never the same again. It had only existed as a mining parish, starting when they sunk the pit in 1900, and had grown up round the pit. Everything was associated with the pit; the colliery youth club, the colliery band, and so on. The parish became almost dead. It was twelve months before the last of the men were got out which had a terrible effect, but on the other hand it did weld the people together. The wonderful thing was the way in which everyone responded – floods of offers of help. People who had money owing to them, the firms cancelled the debts. A lot of the hotel people in Blackpool wrote offering free holidays, and money flowed in from everywhere.'

The vicar explained how the mourners had wanted individual funeral services rather than a huge combined one, so together with the Methodist minister and the Roman Catholic priest, he had organised a day of services, starting at 9 am with a funeral every half an hour in the three churches. He said that three local undertakers shared the funeral arrangements, although Henry Richardson did tell me that Cresswell people were sickened by the many outside firms who were touring the village 'touting for business'.

Walter Burrows, a deputy at Markham colliery, described to me what happened in the 1973 shaft disaster, which happened at 6.20 am on 30 July. He explained that the No 3 shaft was 392 yards deep, and the normal practice was for the winding engine man to apply the brake when the cage was three-quarters of the way down, so that the final descent was nice and steady. The system was that as one cage descended, the cable was connected to another cage, which rose from the pit bottom to the surface. Each cage was a 'double-decker', with men travelling on each of two levels.

Walter told me, 'It was a Monday morning, and we were winding men down underground to get them to work. It was a normal wind until the winding engine man decided to start braking as he normally did, but unfortunately the brake didn't work. Nothing happened; the brake had broken. The result was the cages were going at full speed at that time, and there was no way of stopping them. The cage was estimated as being about 100 yards from the pit bottom, that's where he normally starts braking, and it hit the bottom at full speed. The cage had 29 men on two decks, one above the other.'

It was fortunate that the other cage, the one rising to the surface, was empty on this occasion, but that upward cage still added to the disaster. Walter Burrows continued, 'When the cage hit the bottom, the other cage came up and went through the King system at the top of the shaft. The King system is a process where, should this happen – and an over-wind sometimes happens even in normal circumstances – it immediately cuts the rope and grabs the

The Chesterfield permanent rescue team (top)
and part time rescue team in about 1950. (John Burrows)

cage. It holds it steady, so it can't go back down. The top cage wasn't damaged at all, but the rope fell down the shaft onto the fallen cage. This rope was an inch thick and very heavy, and the woodwork at the top began to topple and fall as well.

'At the pit bottom, we'd got 29 men lying there, some dead, some badly injured, plus all the men who were already underground, and the officials had got to start getting people out. Obviously we couldn't use that shaft, so we had to convert the separate coal-winding shaft immediately to man-riding. Using another shaft, that was a connecting shaft into another colliery, we got the men out that way. Some were obviously dead at that time, and some were seriously injured. We finished up with 18 men who died, and eleven men seriously injured, who never went underground again.

'Some of the eleven went back to work at Markham, but only on the surface, office work, that sort of thing, and others never went back at all. There were other men, not involved in the accident, who also never went underground again. They immediately put their notice in, or asked for surface work. Some went to other collieries that were what they called drift mines, where you could walk down a slope to the coalface. They couldn't face going in a cage down a shaft again. It was a bad, bad day.

'Following the disaster, all sorts of experts had been testing everything, and a public enquiry was called for October. At that time my wife Betty was the manager of the wine department in a local supermarket, and she'd won a week's holiday for two in Majorca, for the amount of sales she had done. We'd never been abroad, but they called the public enquiry for exactly the same week, so I couldn't go. She took a friend with her instead. It was years later that I took my first foreign holiday.

'We had the public inquiry, and fortunately no blame was attached to any individual and thank goodness it wasn't. It was all a mechanical failure, metal fatigue on the braking system. The best thing that came out of it was that every other colliery right throughout the world – and this had never happened anywhere before – every colliery, gold mine, iron mine, all checked their winding equipment. A lot were proved to be using the same system, just relying on one lever to brake, the lever that failed at Markham through metal fatigue.

'The winding man was exonerated; he'd done nothing wrong, but he never went back to work. When he'd put his brake system on he realised there was nothing there, it wasn't going to work. Right at the side of where he was sat, there was a big red button and a sign that said '*In an emergency, press this*'. He did that, yes, he did that, but it turned out to be the worst thing to do, because it cut off the power. If he could have kept his electric power on, he may have been able to slow the winding down, like a car changing gear to slow down. It would never have stopped it but there might not have been so many killed. But he did exactly what he'd been trained to do: in an emergency, press the button.'

Walter Burrows' brother John was vice-president of the area NUM at the time, and he was on his way to an area council meeting in Chesterfield. The first he heard of the shaft disaster was when a lady on the bus said to him, 'What are you doing here? I'd have thought you'd have been at Markham.' When John said that he didn't actually work at Markham, but at the neighbouring Ireland pit, she replied, 'But there's been this terrible disaster at Markham.' 'You what?' he said, aghast. 'Something's happened in the shaft at Markham,' she explained.

Although horrified, John had no choice but to complete his four-mile journey into Chesterfield, where there was 'next to nobody' in the NUM offices. John continues, 'I was told what had happened, went straight down to Markham and helped in the process. Some of the bloody injuries were – I've never seen so many in my life – they were horrific. And some of the bodies, the mutilation was unbelievable. Bodies from the lower cage were about two feet tall, just crushed. Difficult times, awful times.

'I did what I could, and ultimately worked with Pete Heathfield, who, by that time, had become the NUM general secretary, to present the case for the miners at the public enquiry. We had to try and ultimately get some acceptance of responsibility on the part of the Coal Board, so we could get compensation and damages for the men that had been killed or their families. Because without any acceptance of responsibility, they don't just pay people out for the sake of it. There has to be some proof of neglect. A man killed at the pit without acceptance of neglect, his family just got £3,000, it was nothing. And it's still not that much better now. I tried many times to get that raised. I got it up to £6,000 ultimately, but it's still nothing for a man's life.

'Because, he was Markham-based, our Walt had to go along with the branch secretary to the houses of the men that had been killed. He always hated it. How do you tell a young woman that her husband's not coming home? When I was the NUM compensation agent, when fatalities occurred, I had to do that, it was part of the job. Sometimes going with the coppers, turning up on the doorstep with a copper. People knew why we were there and were breaking down before we'd even told them. That was a particularly difficult time.'

Austin Fairest, a NUM official based in Chesterfield, confirmed to me the heartbreak of having to tell a miner's wife that her husband had been killed in the pit. One of his duties as a NUM representative was to accompany a Coal Board official and often a nurse, and on one occasion, on such a terrible errand, he called at the home of a family to tell them that their husband and father was dead. The man was not just a fellow worker, but also one of Austin's drinking companions. 'When we knocked at the door, the man's 14-year-old daughter, answered. She said her mum had nipped up to the shop. When the woman turned the corner and saw us, she immediately knew something awful had happened. "Is it bad?" she asked, and Austin had to say, 'He'll not be coming home, Doreen.'

Austin talked about the trauma of having a friend killed in a pit accident. He claimed that he always felt a strange change in the atmosphere and knew something bad had happened, even before being told of a fatality. After a death, a colliery was 'locked down', no one being allowed to enter or leave the pit. One of the reasons for this, he explained, was to prevent men going home,

The damaged cage and twisted winding rope from the
Markham shaft disaster of 1973. (Cliff Williams)

because news of the death would be all round the community before the dead man's family had been informed.

As a fitter, John Burrows had the job of putting right the faults that had led to the Markham shaft disaster. He was keen to make a good job of it, but his colleagues did not always appreciate his thoroughness.

He says, 'Ultimately I was finding out the technical reasons why it had happened, and I was able to understand it because I'd got the mechanical background. And then being involved in putting in place the statutory processes to stop it happening again, and actually working on the jobs that had to be done to stop it happening at every other shaft in the country. And thinking, Crikey, I'm doing this and I've seen the results if it's not done properly. And getting criticised by some of my mates for saying, "Look, there's no short cuts on this job. If it takes us until nine o'clock in the morning, we're doing this all night." I'd seen the results. They'd not seen it, I had. That was another difficult time.'

At the time I was talking to John Burrows, there had been an accident in a coal mine in the USA, where the relatives had been told that all the trapped men were alive, only to discover the next day that actually all but one had died. Referring to that incident, John added, 'I tell you what, we've had a few tears recently, looking at what's going off in America, understanding it, what's happened. I can even understand how the wrong information has got to them. Not excusing it, but in the midst of all that dilemma, a wrong interpretation of one word can lead to what everybody's hoping to hear anyway, expectations being totally raised, and all done off the back of a word. But twelve colliers killed again, underground, and I had a few tears listening to it.'

Chapter 7

'An Interesting Character'

Many of the ex-miners I spoke to wanted to tell me about characters they had met down the pit, comrades with strong personalities, people with eccentric behaviour. Roy Astle first told me about a Scottish miner whose nickname was 'Tiger', and Roy advised me to ask Ron Wain more about him, as Ron had worked with Tiger over a long period and knew him well.

When I did as Roy had suggested, Ron laughed and replied, 'Oh, you mean Johnnie Campbell. He was a little Scotsman. I was working on the rip at Donisthorpe when I first came into contact with Johnnie. He wasn't one of the original three of us working on the rip, but one of us took ill so they sent Johnnie. Well, in those days it was always hydraulic chocks. We'd got the mushroom chock, known as the Desford chock, and you lifted a ring up and the chock could be moved. When you first come to a rip, you take the guard down and you drill on. Now sometimes it takes two of you, because of the hard rock. So the third one, you send him to start his pack off, out of the waste. Well, first off, he's got to let the chock down and move forward to the next one.

I says to Johnnie, "You know how these work?" "Yes," he says, "I know how they work." Anyway, Mick Dennis was giving me a hand, and we could hear all this banging. Bang, bang, bang, bang, bang. And Mick says, "What's he doing? He's threw his vest off and he's sweating like mad." I said, "Let's get this on, then I'll have a look at him."

'Well, Johnnie was banging away at this chock, trying to knock it out with a hammer, when all he'd got to do was lift the ring. So to learn him a lesson I got hold of this hose and wet him through. I said, "You'll never forget this again." This went on for a whole week! He still used the hammer. I said, "No, you've no need. All you do is pull this up." But you couldn't penetrate.

'But he was as strong as a lion or a tiger. We called him Tiger. He never brought any snap to work with him, because he was in, like, digs. He used to share ours. He would eat anything, and he especially used to like onions. He'd say, "I can eat onion, any sort of onion." I thought I'd teach him a ruddy lesson, so I brought him some bulbs. It's a wonder I didn't kill him, because I learnt afterwards they're poisonous. Anyway, I gave him these bulbs, he got 'em down him. He came to work next day and said, "What did you bloody give me? I stank the house out." Well, same as I said, he'd eat anything. Flip, he was the chock man and he was that busy, most of the time he never had time for his snap. So he gave it to Tiger. But Johnnie got in the habit of eating it before it was offered. We used to say to him, "You can have Flip's snap", so it was our fault really.

'Johnnie always used to tell the tale of when he was back in Scotland. He thought he'd take up boxing. Well, they put him in with a lad that could box, their champion, and he told us, "He knocked me down that many times, and somebody was shouting, *'Get up, John, you can beat him yet!'* and like a fool I kept getting up. I'd get up and he'd knock me down again."

'Johnnie were Johnnie. He was a brilliant drummer, brilliant. He could have played with any band. Also he was one of the nicest blokes I ever met. You know, his feelings for others. He used to put hisself on one side. He'd help anyone. He was a brilliant chap.

Johnnie never missed out on anybody that had passed away who'd been at Donisthorpe. If there was a funeral, he'd turn up. He'd be there.'

Ron went on to say that pit characters were not restricted to colliers but were also to be found amongst the management. 'You had some characters in managers. Now Ern Bosworth, he was one of the longest serving. He was above 20 years at Gresley, him and the undermanager. But anyway, I was on this long haul Dosco machine, and I was the only one who knew anything about it. I was set on because I'd overhauled two at the workshop so I knew all about them. And it was more money, which I needed because I'd just got married. I was on this machine, and I was working Saturdays and Sundays, and I was the only one at that time, because they'd tightened up. Anyway, after a bit we hit hard coal, it used to knock the machine about. You could guarantee on Monday morning, about ten o'clock, the machine would break down about halfway down the face. And every Monday the manager used to sack me, because the machine had broke down. He'd say, "You've been on that machine all Saturday and Sunday." He'd say, "You're the highest paid bloke at the pit. You're taking more home than the deputies and overmen. You're taking more than the undermanager." His standard saying was, "I'll tell you this, my lad, you're not taking more home than me, because I'm the manager of this colliery." Anyway, he always used to reinstate me, like, after I'd got the machine going.

'I got fed up with this being sacked every Monday, and the manager throwing this "You've been all Saturday and Sunday" in my face. The following weekend I never went to work. On Friday I said to my wife, "I'm not doing Saturday and Sunday." I didn't tell her why. And I never went. Anyway, on Monday, about ten o'clock in the morning the machine broke down. They said, "The manager wants you on the phone." I gets on the phone and he starts off, saying, "You've been on that machine all Saturday and Sunday and ...". I cut him short, and I said, "Hold on a bit, Mr Bosworth, I've not been on that machine all day Saturday and Sunday because I didn't come to work." He was quiet for a bit, then he says, "No, the effing machine's ever likely to break down, there's no weekend maintenance been done on it." He'd got me all roads over it. He was a character, though. He'd eff and blind you, and you could eff and blind back, and you'd got a good relationship. You worked your heart out for him. You put the effort in.'

Ron Wain had another example of a boss who was an interesting character. 'At Stanton Lane, we used to have an undermanager name of Cheadle. Now he'd had come from Cadley in the first place and all the men seemed a bit wary of him. He was a bit of a character, a bit sharp-tongued, but he knew his job. For instance, when the old men used to go and collect their pension, every Friday without fail, he'd take 'em in the canteen and buy them a drink of tea. He'd say, "Now you worked in so-and-so, you worked in that district, what was it like then?" Because we were working on old faces, you see, working in that area. And because he'd talked to the old miners, he knew what we were going to hit, what we were going to find.

'I remember one week, I was on packing and they'd paid us short. Everybody was saying, "I'm short of money, are you going in?" I said, "I'm definitely going in, it's my money." They said, "Tell him we're short." So I went in and said, "Mr Cheadle, I'm short of money, and so are so-and-so and so-and-so. The others all say ..." "Have you come in for yourself or them?" he said. I said, "Chiefly me." He said, "You'll get paid, they won't, it's as simple as that." Anyway, he paid me and he even paid me a bit extra.

'But I learned such a lot off him. When we came across old roads, as very often we did, they were brick-lined. Even where the women had been working, shoving tubs, they were that old, you know, and kids opening and closing the doors, because they'd got the old wooden doors. Really old roads. And you could see where the old pick marks were. Mind you, the roads were only about as tall as that mantelshelf. And when the others went to Stanton Drift, when Stanton Lane pit shut down, we had a main coal drift down by the side, and that was the old road, well, we had to crawl down there on us hands and knees. And I once said to Mr Cheadle, "Look at this road, it's as straight as a dye." He said, "Do you know how they did that? Well, you know when they used to bring the candles down, it used to cast a shadow. That's what was termed shadow-cutting." The shadow was always straight, you see, and the roads were as straight as a dye. He'd built up a store of knowledge from what the old men had told him.'

One of the ex-miners I spoke to, John Burrows, certainly would count as a character himself. When he became a full time NUM official, his first job took him a bit by surprise. He found himself in charge of checking up on the running of the Miners' Welfares. Although these may sound like health centres, they were in fact social clubs owned and run jointly by the Coal Board and the unions, places where the miners could relax and have a drink during the week, and take their families on Saturday nights to watch a show. They also often had football and cricket teams attached to them.

John told me, 'The first thing that happened, Pete Heathfield, the Derbyshire general secretary, fetched me and he says, "The first job thou're responsible for, the newest official always has this, any corruption or fiddling in the Miners' Welfare is thy responsibility to sort 'em out." So I says, "You must be joking. I'm a trade union official, I don't want to run the Miners' Welfares." That's when I began to realise that the Miners' Welfares are the coal industry's social welfare organisation, and they are just as much part of the industry as owt else.

'The first job I had to go to with that, was to my own local Welfare, actually. There was some suggestion that the good old-fashioned favourites – the one-armed bandits – weren't returning as much money as they should do. So I went down this Saturday morning, and in the Welfare as you walk through the door to the bar there was a little alcove that these two one-armed bandits sat in. They'd been pulled out, turned round, doors open, two blokes inside with the doors so that no one could see 'em. I looked over the top and says, "What's you two doing?" because I knew both of them, both branch committee men. They said, "What's it got to with thee?" I says, "I've had complaints about the money not being paid off the one-armed bandits, not making as much as they should." They said, "It's got nowt to do with you," so I says, "Turn 'em round, sit this side, count the buggers out this side. And every week a member from the club comes and sits with you – not the same one, a different one every week – and there's some sheets here, you fill out what you've took out of it and that man signs it to verify that's happened. And a different man every week, mind, because you're not getting one man in the same team as you, splitting the divvy three ways instead of two." Well, they were gonna knock me all over the wall, but I was big enough to look after myself. I said, "Don't start anything because both of you'll get seconds, right?" It didn't come to a physical fight, but it was that sort of atmosphere.

'The takings out of them bandits over the next three months went up by £5,000. With that sort of money there must have been others involved with them. The word spread, and as a consequence, wherever I went into a Welfare, the members assumed I'd gone because there was some fiddling going on. "What's tha come for? What's happening?" But nine times out of ten, I'd not gone for that, I'd just gone in for a pint. But anyway my reputation kept 'em on the straight and narrow.'

You can see, I hope, why I regard John as one of the characters of mining.

Terry Butkeraitis, a Whitwell miner, told me about one of his favourite characters, an old communist named Josh Smith. 'Josh was in his eighties at the time of the 1984-85 strike, but he'd never miss a day's picketing. He used to carry a placard round his neck saying, *Support Your Leaders: Scargill, Heathfield, McGahey*. When I went into the Miners' Welfare in Whitwell during the strike, I used to see this other old chap sat there on his own, on a stool in the bar, and nobody was talking to him. I said to old Josh one day, "How come you don't talk to the old lad there?" Josh replied, "He scabbed on us in the 1926 strike." Josh had had nothing to do with him for nearly 60 years! And that old lad, Josh

*The fun-run at Whitwell to raise funds for striking miners in 1984 –
80-year-old Josh Smith did it on walking sticks! (Terry Butkeraitis)*

Smith, actually did a nine-mile fun-run at the end of the strike to
raise money for the sacked miners and for the Women's
Community Centre. We was sat there for about five hours waiting
for him to finish – all the rest had finished hours before. Josh did
the whole nine miles on his walking sticks, but he did it.'

Chapter 8

'Magnificent Defeat'

The miners' strikes that most people remember are the ones from the 1970s, the Ted Heath era, with its resulting three-day-week and periodic power cuts, and the 1984-85 strike when Margaret Thatcher was the Prime Minister which could not in the end prevent the closure of pits in Derbyshire and all over the country. This led some tabloids to label the miners as 'strike happy' but it should be noted that there were no national strikes at all in the mining industry between 1926 and 1972. There were local disputes, of course, but these were at pit level, and were usually sorted out within a few hours.

The 1926 strike began from a demand from the coal owners (all the pits were privately owned before 1947) and backed by a Royal Commission that all miners should receive a pay cut of at least 13½% and that there should be an hour longer on each shift. This was accompanied by a proposal that the minimum wage agreed in 1924 (which was 33% of the standard wage) should be abolished. The coal owners' proposal was fiercely resisted by the miners and their union. For a period of nine days in May 1926, the TUC backed the miners' fight and the first-ever national general strike was declared. Transport workers, engineers, electricians, printers and many others came out on official strike in support of the miners, but the TUC leaders panicked about their action and surrendered to the government led by Prime Minister Stanley Baldwin, who was fully in support of the coal owners. The miners, however, continued their struggle for another six months, before agreeing to go back to work in November.

The January 1972 strike also was about pay. John Burrows explained, 'From my point of view it was a genuine attempt to get an increase in wages, because at that time the wages were abysmally low. I was looking through some stuff the other day and came across a pay slip of mine from about that time. It was £8.70 for the week, and it wasn't a lot of money.'

Soon after the national miners' strike began, coal rationing was introduced by the government and a three-day week soon hit British industry, with over a million workers laid off. The government set up an enquiry under Lord Wilberforce, which led to a higher pay offer to the miners. 'It was an enquiry that was just a charade if you know what I mean,' John went on, 'but it gave us what we wanted, including a promise of a superannuated pension because that had always been a longstanding argument. A collier retiring at that time at 65, after a full life working in the pit, was getting 30 shillings a week, and it was disgraceful. And from that enquiry we got the promise of a superannuated pension though it didn't come through till '76.'

In November 1973 another strike by the miners (which ended in March 1974 with a substantial pay offer) and other workers led directly to the election of a Labour government under Harold Wilson.

As Area Vice President of the NUM, John was very active in both strikes. 'The 1972 pit strike was a national strike, and it's something that I am immensely proud of, not just of the colliers that took part in it and the way that it was done. I'm also proud of my role as a representative both of the Derbyshire area and particularly of the miners at Ireland colliery. We made a bit of a reputation for oursen' on the picket line. We had little or no

A visit by NUM president Joe Gormley to Donisthorpe in the 1960s.

problem with men going into work at Ireland colliery, so we went and did a token picket there from five o'clock till six o'clock in the morning.

'Then we recognised that it was a bigger problem at Markham – it was a bigger pit and there were more men, and there were deputies, our Walt, for example, and my older brother Ellis, that were being told that they had to go in. And with the intention to stop them from going into work, I took a busload of Ireland men up to Markham. Only a matter of a mile and a half, but I took them up to Markham to help and join in. At that point in time, we were outnumbered by the coppers because the pickets were just Markham and Ireland men.

'I thought this was not good enough, we'd got to get some men in from other pits, so I went to other pits like Whitwell and Renishaw Park and other places, and then I went back to the area council and said, "It's about time we recognised that this is a national dispute. You can't all just stop at your own pits. It's about time people were turning up at Markham and stop this process that's going on, because it's getting quite heavy." The next morning there were literally hundreds of miners from the whole of Derbyshire turned up.

'It were a real battle to stop the deputies, who were not members of the NUM but members of NACODS [National Association of Colliery Overmen, Deputies and Shotfirers]. The NACODS men had ensconced themselves in the ambulance room at Duckmanton, where they'd decided they were going to meet with their full-time official and with the police superintendent and inspector. The police decided on the tactic of marching them down the hill – because it was no use them going individually – they'd march them downhill to the pit with a police escort. But to cut a long story short, they didn't. It was a pitched battle, with policemen being knocked over hedges and garden walls, helmets going up in the air, deputies frightened to death and turning back and going home. And that happened day upon day upon day, until one day the police had brought enough men to say they were going in on this day, and they did.

'I can remember shouting over the police lines to our Walt and to our Ellis, "You'll not always be behind coppers. We're going to meet up face to face. It'll not be the same when we get home and I'll sort thee out," and all that kind of thing. After the strike, relationships between me and the other two lads that were deputies, Ellis and Walt, were a bit strained, but they were still relationships.'

Walter and John now live opposite each other in the same street in Brimington. They are both actively involved in local politics, and are members of the same party.

John had always wanted to become a full-time NUM official. In 1981 he stood against nine other candidates and was elected. 'At the age of 41, I was the youngest full-time officer at that time in the country and it was the first time a craftsman had been elected to that role ever.'

'Anyway, very quickly it built up to the '84 strike. The '84 strike was the most difficult twelve or maybe 18 months of my life, in terms of starting off with the full glory of people thinking we're going on strike again, it'll be another '72 or '74. I always said it'd never be that, because there were too many factors against us. But events took place as they took place.'

The 1984 miners' strike was not about pay or even conditions. It was a fight to prevent the Conservative government led by Margaret Thatcher closing down pits, as a prelude to having just a handful of very profitable collieries that could then be privatised. The government and Coal Board had planned their strategy, building up massive coal stocks at power stations before starting to shut down collieries, to provoke the strike. John continued, 'Some older colliers were saying, "These young 'uns will never do what we did." And I said, "They're no different to what you were. They're colliers that are looking after their bloody jobs and they'll be just as good if not better." And in the first two or three months that was proved beyond doubt. They were another generation of fighting, politically motivated, job-preservation miners. I was 100% proud of 'em, from men to lads.

The headquarters of the National Union of Mineworkers in Chesterfield.

'I went out every morning at five o'clock to various picket lines, did that sort of thing, then went to work – my union work – at eight o'clock, trying to sort money out, trying to sort problems out, getting involved in discussions and negotiations. They were twelve, 18-hour days, non-stop. It was very traumatic, very stressful.'

Once again, the Burrows family was divided. 'Our Les, another brother, was a member of the British Association of Colliery Management at that time, and BACAM were working. And NACODS were working, against our best wishes, so Walt and Ellis, they were working. It was extremely difficult, and family relationships were strained. I'd got the best woman in the bloody world, who put up with everything, because I was coming home and bringing all my problems home and wanting to fall out with her because I couldn't fall out with anybody else. Best woman in the world, and she put up with all that. Kids, I loved my kids but I hardly seen 'em. At that time I'd got a black Labrador cross bitch that, didn't matter what time of day or night I came home, I used to put her on her lead and walk the fields. I'd just walk and I talked to her. And she'd stop and look at me and think, What're you talking about, you silly bugger? That dog helped keep me sane.

'And from all the glory and glamour of the first two or three months, everybody fully solid, after six months it was clear to me that we were in a different ball game. By that time we'd got McGregor on the scene.'

Ian McGregor was an American industrialist brought in by the government to run the Coal Board and specifically to defeat the miners, led by NUM President, Arthur Scargill.

John continued, 'It was clear that Thatcher was prepared to spend anything necessary to lick us. It wasn't just us she were licking, it was working people whether they were trade unionists or not, it was a class struggle. And I'd always been into that, all my life, and I always will be. And that signalled to me that to win it, it was going to be extremely difficult. I'd had feedback from

---

Picketing the mines in 1984 often led to pitched battles with the police, many of whom were drafted in from all over the country. This was the scene at Cadley Hill in South Derbyshire. (Magic Attic Archives)

Peter Heathfield (the NUM General Secretary) and Scargill – who I knew like family because I'd worked that closely with 'em over a long period of time – that McGregor was working to settle. There was an occasion where they'd gone into negotiations, they'd got agreement, he'd come to settle. But then McGregor left the room. Peter Heathfield had also left the room to go to the toilet and he saw McGregor on the phone, a public phone, talking to Maggie [Thatcher]. He later claimed he was ringing his sister, but as soon as he got back in to the negotiations, all that had been agreed and settled, just a matter of sorting it, everything was thrown out. She'd obviously said to him, "You're not settling under any circumstances. They're not beaten yet, and it will only stop when they will admit they're beaten." And that happened several times.

'They were very difficult times, and after six months, the lads – well, the men, but I always call them the lads, I don't know why – the lads, the workforce, were beginning to struggle and suffer with mortgages, threats of reclaiming properties. We were doing everything to sort that out, fetching in branch officials to do surgeries so that anybody who'd got that bother could go along to 'em. Setting up the process, getting in touch with banking trade unions who were advising us how best to avoid repossession, by simply paying the interest. If you talk to these companies early enough, they will not go into repossession as long as you pay the interest. They know that at some time the dispute will be over, you'll be able to pay the capital off over a longer period of time. We staved off dozens upon dozens of repossessions simply by the union being able to help out financially.

'We then got these two scab colliers who took us to court on the basis that we'd had a ballot in Derbyshire and the vote had not been a sufficient majority, and therefore the strike in Derbyshire was illegal. They took us to the High Court in London – what a bloody experience for a humble collier's lad in the dock in the High Court, with wigs and papers and everything that was going off, and being told that I was fraudulently using money, and all them sort of things. I just took it on the chin, I just thought, well, the worst thing that can happen is they put me in prison. There's better men than me for far less principle been put in prison in the past. I'll be another one. I took it on the chin, but the stresses build up and you don't realise over a period of time how much the stress gets at you. Ultimately, the judgement went against us but the judge, whilst applying the law, had got enough common sense to know that the only reason we were spending the money was to stop colliers and their kids from starving to death. He said we'd got to stop using the money for strike purposes and we could only spend it for legitimate union reasons. Which completely stymied us because we'd got no money then. Well, there was plenty of money left but we'd got no money to spend on the workforce.

'My job then became one of trying to find some funds, going to every other major trade union – because at that time the national NUM funds had been sequestered and they were in financial difficulties – talking to high profile trade unionists, and begging for money. And getting money. The stories in the papers at that time about £50,000 in cash in carrier bags were speculation on their part, but they were bloody true. I was travelling all over the country with carrier bags with anything between £60,000 and £100,000 in money. The money wasn't given to us, but loaned, that had ultimately got to be repaid. And keeping it away from any of the official financial activities of the trade union, because these other trade unions would have been in trouble had it been common knowledge that they were helping us. Keeping the books – not cooking them, keeping them – so that ultimately, at the end of whatever was going to happen, we could make sure that everything was repaid. And using that money to help colliers to live and to survive.

'Difficult times, easy to talk about now, but difficult times when a collier and his wife, 24 or 25-years-old, come in to your office, both of 'em crying because the bailiffs are at the door, and you'd not got any money to help 'em to do owt. And he's saying, "I shall have to go back to work," and I'm saying, "Don't do that, you're going to be in worse bother than ever." Because the then NCB area director set up a process to get men back to work, it became impossible to stop the gentle, steady flow of men going back. And after twelve months, with the same sort of problem happening in other areas, the strike began to fragment.

'It really hit me when talking to my equivalents in the South Wales area who, up to that point, had been 100% solid, who said, "We've got to find a formula to get back to work, because we're not having what's happening in your area and in Yorkshire where dribs and drabs of men are going back to work with no dignity left, being called names after they'd been on strike for ten, eleven, some of them twelve months, being called names and labelled scabs in the same way as men who'd never had a day off work were labelled. We're not having that. If we're going back to work, we're all going back together."

'Ultimately that led to a national conference being called at which we had to make a decision whether we were going to call for a continuation of the strike or a return to work to preserve the bloody dignity of the workforce. And when the votes were cast, there was a majority of two votes in favour of going back to work, much to Arthur's and Peter's disgust. At that time there were a large number of sacked miners outside the conference who recognised that a successful conclusion to the strike was their only hope of getting back to work, and that had just disappeared. They were up in arms, and Arthur went out to them and was critical of people who had voted to go back to work. While I wasn't one of them, I did think it was right to go back to work for the dignity of the trade union members. Everybody else had buggered off, frightened to death, but I didn't. I went out with Arthur and argued why it was right we went back to work and promised that I would do everything I could to get them sacked men their jobs back. That became my priority after the strike. I wasn't successful with all of 'em, but I got a damned good many of 'em back to work.

'And from that, it went on until all the pits were ultimately shut – that's well noted in history. No matter what Arthur says about the strike being a magnificent victory, it wasn't. It was a magnificent defeat. The strike was lost.'

Paul Liversuch does not agree. He believes that because the strike politicized people and made them fight for their heritage, it was a success. One man who had been sacked by the Coal Board was Terry Butkeraitis from Whitwell colliery. His crime was to occupy the headstocks at Whitwell pit, to prevent two scab miners going down the shaft. Terry, his brother John, and three other pickets, spent two days on top of the building, and the men were sacked for 'criminal damage'. When I asked him what damage had been done, he explained that they had painted slogans on the walls proclaiming *Under New Management* and *Victory '84*.

Terry spent of lot of his time during the strike raising money for the miners. He told me, 'We were going down to London, raising money, going to meetings, spreading the word, bringing money back, sustaining our own community that way. Because even though we were getting a lot of bad press from October onwards, the ordinary people leading up to Christmas still felt for us and still supported us financially, as much as they could. I went on the streets of London, I went to meetings, I did everything possible.

Terry Butkeraitis (centre) and fellow strikers on Whitwell shaft top.
All five were sacked for criminal damage.

Committed miners from Whitwell. (Terry Butkeraitis)

'We had a fund where we could help towards gas bills, electric bills, even mortgages. We could pull solicitors in to send letters, saying they were striking miners and so forestall on lots of things. All that was work that happens behind the scenes, that you have to do. And as branch president I'd got 850 men, NUM members, that I felt a little bit more responsible for at times. For example, I went on a mass picket, and I was on a picket line where one or two of them had got arrested for pushing, scrapping with policemen, whatever it were, and I felt a little bit aggrieved and sad that the actions that I'd been part of had resulted in some of them being in jail. It's a bitter pill to swallow but you have to swallow it.

'At Christmas, we managed to have a do in Whitwell to celebrate, we called it a Pickets' Ball. Beer was quite cheap and everybody found a couple of quid to go and spend on beer. We got dressed as pickets, we'd got flat caps and all us badges on. And even though we were facing defeat – we knew that, if we looked deep down – we still celebrated.

'We certainly didn't go down without a fight, we certainly kept us dignity and us pride. It weren't about wages, and I think History has proved we were right. We followed our leaders. We don't think Arthur [Scargill] ever told us a lie. I've met Arthur on numerous occasions, we have a reunion every year, we have a few speakers on and we still have a bit of a pickets' ball, even now to this day. We hold it locally, down the road in Mansfield, and people come from all over the country.

'It's like the Durham Miners' Gala, except it's in a building. There's about 500 turn up. It's meeting old friends again. We get dressed up with flat caps, and reminisce, like old wartime stories. And believe you me, it was a war.'

Chapter 9

A Woman's Viewpoint

Most of the memories in this book are those of men, because the pit was a very male community. Of course there was once a time when women – and children – were employed in mines, pulling wagons and opening the heavy doors, but for more than a hundred years working underground in a coal mine had been restricted to men.

However, during the hard times – especially the 1984-85 strike – women did come into their own. Wives and daughters of striking miners first got involved in running kitchens – what were once called soup kitchens – providing wholesome food for the miners and their families. Soon however, they found themselves attending rallies, and even travelling to other areas to address meetings, to explain what the strike was all about. One of these was Sherryl Stansbury from Whitwell.

Sherryl comes from a mining family, and she told me about her dad, Dennis Reynolds. 'My dad was a miner. He had a bad accident at Whitwell, and they had to give him a tracheotomy at the pit bottom. I think a chain had fallen on the belt or something. They usually say a big bloke comes off best in an accident. This

The Eckington Women's Action Group.

time they said if he had been a big bloke it'd have killed him instantly, but luckily he was only a little bloke. He was in hospital for ages and ages. He was also on the cage when that went down at Whitwell – this was before the Markham one – and he did his knees. I can still remember him shuffling up steps on his bum.'

When I asked Sherryl about her connection with Whitwell in 1984, she told me, 'We lived in Whitwell, but my husband Fred worked at Shireoaks pit. But obviously during the strike, he couldn't afford to travel to Shireoaks each day, because we were short of money, so he went and joined up with the Whitwell pickets. He was born and bred in Whitwell and he knew everybody, so he joined their strike.'

I asked Sherryl if she had been active in earlier strikes, and she said, 'No, just the '84 one. We set up a women's group at a centre in Whitwell, about eight of us, who helped in the kitchen. There was Sheila Turner, Debra Howell, Margaret Belfit, Melanie Ward, Sally Beavers, Wendy Allcroft, Joan Pressley and me. Sometimes Yvonne Streets and Sandra Richardson as well.

'We'd only got a four-ring cooker, and at one time we were cooking for 200, I think, because at the beginning of the strike, everybody come in. We gave them potatoes, meat, something to start with, then something after. They had a three course meal. The premises belonged to the council so we didn't have to pay to use the place. We managed all the cooking on those four rings.

'We went in the morning, cooked the dinner, then got everything cleaned up. Then when the schools were off on holiday, they let us use the local school kitchen. It was much better there, with washing up for all that many. It was equipped for all the kids, a sterilizer and everything, so it was spot on. That

The Whitwell Women's Support Group at Whitwell Miners' Welfare –
Sheila Turner, Sherryl Stansbury, Debra Howell, Margaret Belfit,
Melanie Ward, Sally Beavers, Wendy Allcroft and Joan Pressley.
(Sherryl Stansbury)

was only when the school was off, like. We kept up the kitchen until they went back to work, for as long as people wanted to drift in, but the numbers were going down at the end.

'We finished up going down London, and I think it opened us eyes, because a lot of the women had never done things like that. I'd hardly been out of Whitwell, really, except for holidays at the miners' camp at Skeggy or the pub outing to Cleethorpes. When we got down there in London, we went to different people who put us up. We went all over, collecting money. We needed money to keep the food coming in, to feed the miners and their families. We went to the British Airways workers, doing a speech there. We went to the Elephant and Castle, stood outside with some of the Manton miners, giving leaflets out, giving speeches, going round collecting food. It was red hot, the weather. You can stand there with the leaflets, you can't give them out, people have to take them off you. And they said, "Don't walk up and down the street, don't move," so all one side was sunburnt because we just stood there.

'A group of us, we went to London quite a few times. There were four of us that were really active: there was Sheila Turner, Sang's wife, there were Debbie Howell, and Wendy Allcroft, she's Sheila's daughter, and me. That was the main core that went down to London. We'd never done anything like this before, it were a new thing, but I mean, to sustain ourselves, we had to raise money to keep the kitchen working.'

When I asked Sherryl how she felt about having to address a roomful of people during a meeting, she admitted to being very nervous. 'That opened us eyes, yes. From a little country village like Whitwell, down into London, it were a bit nerve wracking. We took it in turns to give the speeches, like. I did one at what do they call it, is it BAFTA? No, BECTU? Anyway, all the film people. I was terrified. I had a quick scribble down, because I mean I'd never put anything together like that before. I think I've still got the speech somewhere. I just stood up and did it. We went to Hounslow, Wandsworth, Battersea. There were plenty of people who put us up, we still send Christmas cards to 'em now.

A rally of Women's Support Groups at Chesterfield in March 1985.

Another time we went to Greenham Common, where we spent the night camping, and the day collecting money.

'On one visit we went and planted a tree at a school, and we had to address the kids. I think that was more harrowing than addressing an adult meeting. They were just sat there, they hadn't got a clue what we were on about. You couldn't say too much because they were never going to understand what we were, not in London, were they? But it was all right, and we planted the tree.'

In some areas, women who were active during the 1984 strike found that their husbands became resentful at their new-found confidence and independent thought. However, when I asked Sherryl whether the husbands of the women in the Whitwell Action Group had supported them when they began to branch out, going to London and giving talks, she told me that they certainly did, 'Sang, Sheila's husband, and Fred were very supportive of us.'

Terry Butkeraitis, the branch president of the Whitwell NUM during the strike, paid his own tribute to the work of the Whitwell women. 'The Women's Action group in Whitwell was superb. Some farmers were on board and they'd give a trailer-load of cabbages, and some local butchers would give meat, because they knew after the strike we'd all have to work together anyway. The miners quickly learnt that they could go into Clowne, another village nearby, and have a breakfast, call in at Whitwell and have their lunch, then call in at Cresswell and have their tea! They'd got a nice merry-go-round where they got fed, and fed pretty well really.'

Chapter 10

South Derbyshire and the Strike

Although the miners in North Derbyshire were fully behind the 1984 strike, seeing it as a battle for the future of mining, it was different in the smaller South Derbyshire coalfield.

Paul Liversuch explained: 'South Derbyshire miners had supported the 1972 strike, in fact it was quite strong support. I was very active in '72. We spent long cold days picketing. All the pits shut. I picketed my own pit, Donisthorpe, and made sure nobody went in. South Derbyshire as a whole was very strong. We picketed the pits and we picketed the open cast site at Albert village. The Transport & General (TGWU) drivers used to come up to us and ask, "What do you want us to do? Do you want us to go straight by?" Some of the police at that time realised that if we were defeated by the government they could be next in the firing line, and they were very co-operative with us. The days were bitter cold but Johnnie Campbell, 'Tiger', he'd walk all the way from Newhall to Donisthorpe to go on the picket line. The landlord of the local pub would send us a drink out. The pit manager allowed us to go on the yard to pick up the scrap wood and waste material to burn in the picket line brazier. In fact, there was a good atmosphere there, with the same humour and comradeship like we had down the pit.

'By 1984 it was very different – it was more political. South Derbyshire NUM had a right-wing local leadership that wanted to have a cosy life with the Coal Board, and they didn't want us to rock the boat. But there were those of us who were not prepared to pay that price. Our loyalty should be first and foremost to our members and to keeping pits open. We had had a lot of battles over the introduction of a bonus scheme, which some of us knew could lead to more accidents. It would have also split the union, with some areas earning more than others. Although the union voted against it, South Derbyshire and Nottinghamshire went against the democratic decision. And that was where the rot set in.

'When it came to the 1984 strike Nottinghamshire and South Derbyshire opposed the national union. They were always loath to take any action, so when Kent, Durham, Yorkshire, Wales, North Derbyshire and all those areas came out on strike, the pits in South Derbyshire kept on working. It was quite plain to many of us that the plan of the government was to break the NUM.

'There was some picketing of the pits and I never crossed a picket line myself, but that was only for a few days. I decided that I would have to carry on working, not because I didn't believe in the cause, but because we'd had a ballot over going on strike. The local union leaders had put no recommendation on the ballot sheet, deliberately given no advice – which was unheard of. No leadership was given, and the majority vote was not to strike. It was very much against my own feelings but I felt I had to accept the decision and go to work. It was a real battle with my conscience. I decided to send donations to the striking miners in other areas.

'After the end of the strike, there was another vote in South Derbyshire, this time to set up the UDM (Union of Democratic Miners). All the NUM money and even our NUM building went to the UDM. I still think those of us in opposition had the majority, but we were never shown the votes. I mean, some pits

The UDM (Union of Democratic Mineworkers) building in Swadlincote.

were registering 100% majority, and you just never get that in any ballot. I believe we had the majority. You might say, well, you're bound to say that, but if you add up the members of COSA (the union for colliery office workers) and the NUM we had the majority. You can't prove it but we had suspicions of it.'

The breakaway of the UDM was an exact replica of what happened after the 1926 strike, when George Spencer, a Notts MP, founded the Nottingham & District Miners' Industrial Union. This union was anti-strike and pro-mine owners, and while it called itself 'moderate', it was always referred to as 'a scab union' by the majority of miners. The name of George Spencer was one that was reviled in NUM circles.

Paul Liversuch went on, 'I fought very hard to keep the NUM going round here, and I became the president of the South Derbyshire NUM after the split. All the men had been automatically put into the UDM but a lot of them were not happy with that and came back into the NUM. We managed to get NUM members in all the pits and even in Pits Rescue. It was my privilege to steer it through for a very difficult period when we had no funds and no building to meet in, so we were meeting in pub rooms until the national president of the union got us a place where we could have our offices. We had to go through a very difficult period, but at the end of the day we stood firm. Even to this day. The good thing about it is, I do the compensation claims for the NUM miners in South Derbyshire so the work still goes on, even though the coalfield has disappeared. The wonderful thing is being part of something you believe in.'

Paul, like many others, paid a personal price for his life-long commitment to his fellow miners. 'There was a price to pay, of

The effigy is thought to be of George Spencer, founder of the 'moderate' or 'scab' union in 1926, at Bolsover. Note the would-be junior Robin Hoods! (Cliff Williams)

course, there always is. My father completely wrote me off, and left me nothing. It was only when he was dying that he eventually agreed to make it up. He hated what I stood for. He never spoke or had anything to do with me for years. He was a Conservative and he literally hated me and he hated Arthur Scargill. He totally opposed what I did, but that was a price to pay and I don't ever regret it. I feel with no amount of arrogance that we were right. I believe that time has proved we were right. Some people, I don't know how they can live with themselves for what they did. I did something that I believed in. That's the main thing. I can live with myself.'

Chapter 11

Pit Humour

As in any workplace, the miners developed their own humour. In difficult and sometimes dangerous conditions, having a laugh becomes a vital way of keeping things in proportion. The police and ambulance service have their own methods of joking their way through traumatic situations that would have the rest of us screaming or weeping. When the pit humour is allied to a dry Derbyshire wit, it can become something unique.

Austin Fairest told me of one incident, in a Derbyshire drift mine. Most of the men on his shift were waiting on the paddy cart, when the last man arrived. He wandered in saying, 'You know, I'm sure I've forgot something.' Austin thought he might have forgotten his snap or even his water bottle but the men looked up to see the latecomer was wearing his boots, his helmet and his cap lamp – but nothing else. Apart from his head and his feet, the man was stark naked. 'And it was a bloody cold mine,' Austin added.

Sometimes the humour was aimed at authority – often in the form of the deputy. Walter Burrows recalls one such incident at Markham. 'My job as a deputy was to set men off to work, record

Williamthorpe colliery, before and after modernisation. (John Burrows)

who'd come and check whether they'd got the right equipment and the lamps were working correctly. When I'd done all that they got on the man-rider which took them to each of the workings. While they were riding in, I had to go back into the local pit-bottom cabin and do a lot of paperwork, then send it up to the time office. By the time I'd done this, the men should have been at work, and I followed them in on another man-rider. When I went out this time the man-rider was nowhere to be seen, and I spoke to the engine driver and said, "What's up?" And he said, 'Well, they've only got halfway down and they've stopped me so I don't know what's up."

'So I had to walk about 800 yards, halfway down the roadway, to find the men had stopped the cars because just in front of them was some water. It was what we called a swillet, which meant it was an undulation in the roadway where the water kept gathering. There was a pump there and the previous shift had failed to pump the water out. The men couldn't go through, their legs would have been underwater. I said, "Well, hasn't anybody been and pumped it out?" because the pump was in the middle of the water. No! So I had to take my boots and socks off, roll my trousers up well above my knees and wade in and start the pump. It took ten or 15 minutes to pump the water out.

'The mistake I'd made when I'd took my boots and socks off, I'd left them there, so when I eventually came back and said, "Right, we're all right now", I couldn't find them. What the men'd done, they'd hid 'em, and for about ten to 15 minutes they'd got me running about looking for my boots and socks before they eventually said they're here, before we could go on. There was little things like that, it was pit life. It was okay and we enjoyed it though, took it in us stride.'

Paul Liversuch who worked in the South Derbyshire coalfield, at Donisthorpe Colliery adds, 'It wasn't a miserable job, it was a job where people had antics and played tricks on people. In pits people rubbed up and people had nicknames, and there were humorous times. It wasn't sad times. The banter were terrific. You never had a dull moment. There was one chap going out with a girl who was 20 years his younger, so he was regularly bantered on. They'd say why on earth has she fell for you, Barry, you're too ugly to have somebody like that. They used to pull his leg something wicked. You'd wind somebody up but it very rarely get out of control.'

However, Paul found that during times of trouble, especially during the '84 strike period, the banter did have an edge to it. 'When we had the problems in the pits and the disputes, particularly the last dispute, and they set the breakaway union up, I was never referred to as Paul. My name was always "Scargill", or "Arthur". It was "Arthur" if it was endearment or "Scargill, you red bastard" if it was anti. I used to say to Arthur Scargill, "Do you know we've both got the same name?" I'd always be bantered on that. The official on nights always called me Red Ken. He'd shout across the yard, "Red Ken!". You'd have to put up with that sort of banter, if you know what I mean.'

Paul had mentioned nicknames, and Ron Wain told me, 'There's been a good many books wrote about Derbyshire, but I tell you what's never been mentioned – the slang names. There were a lot of Parkers, you see, working in the pit, so there was Shinpad Parker, Squarker Parker, Doc Parker, Fatty Parker, Squeaker Parker, Roper Parker, all these, and there was Woody Staley and Puff Whetton. The reason why, if there were a lot of Parkers, you'd say, "Ay, I bumped into Squarker," and they knew instantly which one you meant. There was nothing detrimental. There was another one we used to call Knowledge, because he seemed to know everything about everything.

'There was a lot of different names at the pit, and also for the tools that we used. And each pit had its own vocabulary. The wood that we used on top of the steel props or anything like that we called caps, which fitted on top of the props. But in Chesterfield, I can remember Swaffer, he came from Chesterfield, he used to call them bells, I don't know why. And a shovel was called a banjo, that was a round shovel. And there were tadgers, they were picks with a blade you needed to tadge out the wooden props. Working at Stanton Lane, it was only a small pit of about

150 men if that, at the pit, and the wooden props we used time and time again, so we had to tadge 'em out – knock them out from where they were no longer needed – so they could be used again. You had to watch you didn't ruin 'em by tadging 'em through the middle.'

John Burrows told me of one trick played on a miner. 'We were doing a job in Ireland pit bottom. After the shaft accident at Markham, every sump had to have these massive rubber Oleo buffers. They were big pieces of compound rubber, on steel top and bottom plates, that had to be sat onto girders so that if the chair actually came down, at least there was a bit of contraction. I'd been working on preparation for about three months, and they gave me three colliers to work with me on this job.

'One of the colliers is a youth who I still knock about with, my life-long best mate, and of course he was full of mischief, as we all were. Part of the game. And we got talking about the pit bottom ghost. We did it purposely because we knew that Albert, the guy that was the onsetter working the signal bells, was a little bit iffy and concerned. We built it up a bit, until he says, "I tell you I've worked here over 30 years, I've worked even before we had cap lamps, and there's no ghosts here." We answered him, saying, "We're telling you there's definitely a ghost in the sump."

'The next day, on this level that we're at, there were massive heaps of hoses and cotton rope and all the stuff that were part of the game, inch diameter cotton rope. And there were three levels where we were working, and the next day Waggy Weston brought a little bit of light fishing wire, dropped it from the top level to where we were working and just tied it to the end of one of the cotton ropes. At that time there was no mains electricity, everybody was on cap lamps because the electricians were doing their job. We were talking about this ghost, and Albert's working the bells, when I said, "Eh up, he's here," meaning the ghost. I said that because Waggy's pulling this bit of fishing wire, and a coil of rope started to rise beautifully. Albert looked away, did a double take – the traditional double take – then disappeared up the slit away from the pit. It took us two days to get him to come

Minorca pit at Measham in 1981. (SDMPG)

back down to work with us. He'd come back in but he wouldn't go up the slit. But he never knew that we'd set it up like that.'

'And talking of ghost stories, whilst I was delegate at Ireland pit, the lads working the plane on the tackle were refusing to go for it because they said there was a ghost on the plane. This was just after a guy who was a fitter had been taken round a drive and got killed, and the word was that his ghost was on the plane. And it was serious stuff, the lads were refusing to go on the tackle, and they said they knew there was a ghost there, they'd seen it.

'The manager came and said, "What are we going to do about it?" I said, "Somebody's got to go and walk the plane, just to show how to do it." Of course there's a bit of trepidation about this, even from me, and he says, "I'm not keen on that!"

'I says, "Come on, we've got to go." So we set off, we went on the cars to the top of the plane, started walking down, just walking, talking, looking. Eventually this light flashed. We'd given instructions that there was to be nobody on the plane until we'd shifted from the top right through to the bottom. And yet this light flashed in the distance, and the manager said, "There's somebody on the plane there, but it only flashed on and off." Because you can see a light before you can see a man. So he says, "That's a bit strange." So we had a bit more trepidation.

'We went a bit further, carefully looking in front. Eventually it flashed again. I said, "There's somebody down there acting about, trying to frighten us." So we sharpened the pace up. Almost the same distance again, it flashed. I said, "There's something not right about that." It were very eerie, remember we're in pitch black. We've got two lamps, everybody's been instructed not to be there, and still this light's flashing. Eventually, with a lot of fear in both of us, the manager says, "I wish I'd never agreed with thee to come here." I said, "I wish I'd never suggested it." Eventually we get close enough to this piece of switchgear to see its got in it what we call a bull's eye. That's a piece of very thick toughened glass to protect the amp meter. The flashing was our spot lamps reflecting off the bull's eye. And I tell you what, we were frightened, we were frightened.'

Finally, another couple of stories from Austin Fairest. The first was of a miner who came in grumbling that his wife had bought 'one of them newfangled microwaves', and how he didn't get on with it like with the old stove. His mates were surprised, as their wives had taken to using them with no problems. 'Well,' he explained, 'I put my boots in to warm for a bit and they were rubbish when I got them out.'

The second concerned a character he met while working at High Moor Pit. This was a Scottish miner of rugged appearance and uncertain temper. His gnarled knuckles indicated that he had been in many a fight. The man had a scary reputation as a hard man, and his workmates were careful never to cross him or upset him in any way. The only problem was that his accent was so strong that no one knew what he was saying, so people usually just nodded and agreed with him. On one occasion, Austin told me, the tough Scot told a joke and his listeners roared with laughter. One Derbyshire miner, younger than the others and a bit naïve, announced, 'I don't get it.' One of his older and wiser workmates leaned over and growled, 'Tha will do if tha doesn't laugh!'

Walter Burrows' story occurred because of a misunderstanding at home. He explained, 'I didn't talk to Betty much about my work as a deputy, we just talked about family and what we were doing, so mining terms were something she wasn't used to. All collieries in those days worked three shifts, days, afternoons and nights. I came home one day and we'd had a terrible shift, because of what we used to call a wait break. Usually, in the area left behind where we'd took the coal out, the gob or the waste used to break off and fall down on a regular basis. But in this instance, for two or three days it hadn't fallen, so when it did come, instead of dropping in small blocks it held together. When it eventually fell, it came all over the actual face where we were working, and we had a hell of a job. It was awful. When I came home this particular day, I must have looked fed up. Betty says, "Has something gone wrong?" and I said, "Yes, we've had a wait-break." Because she didn't understand mining terms, all she said was, "Well, couldn't you mend it?"

The dry Derbyshire pit humour can surface even in the most unlikely circumstances. John Burrows told me of an incident that happened during the 1974 strike. John had taken a bus-load of Derbyshire pickets to Saltley Coke depot. One of his men was arrested, and after the picketing, John took the bus round to the police station to see if he could collect him. John told me, 'I went in the police station, fetched him out and said, "What did they arrest you for?" "Throwing a missile," he said. I said, "You weren't throwing a stone, were you?" He said, "No, a meat pie! I didn't even get to eat my meat pie, so I threw it in sheer frustration." I said, "Haven't tha had any snap, then?" and he said, "Aye, they gave me a sandwich." I asked him what was in it and he replied, "I think it was probably seagull".'

Chapter 12

The End of an Era

Now that every pit in Derbyshire has been closed, the iconic sight of a pit head with its winding wheel has virtually disappeared. Many former mines have become factory estates, still providing local employment, though on a much smaller scale. In some places, the old winding wheels have been incorporated in monuments to the glories of the good old days of mining. In Swadlincote, one former mine site is now a ski slope, attracting those who wish to practise dry skiing before going off to Switzerland, Scotland or Scandinavia to tackle the snow slopes there.

I thought it would be interesting to discover what the miners whose memories have featured in this book did after their traditional means of employment had gone. Some, including Roy Astle, retired of course, because of their age or because of poor health. Others, the younger men, had to find other work, and for some it wasn't easy. John Burrows had built up a reputation as a full time NUM official, very active in the 1984-5 strike. This did him no harm in his union job, but proved a handicap when he was looking for work elsewhere. John told

The former Sharpe's Pottery in Swadlincote, now a heritage centre.

me, 'By 1991 all the pits had gone, so there was no further justification for four full time union officials and I was ultimately made redundant. Then I had to find a job, I had to find work. I was a relatively young man with a family, mostly grown up, but I'd got to have some income. And for ten months, after being made redundant, I was applying for a whole variety of jobs. As soon as I went into the interview and they knew my background as an NUM official, they didn't see me, they saw Arthur Scargill, the then bogey-man. I failed to get many jobs that I was more than capable of doing, probably over qualified in terms of experience and technical ability, failed to get them on the back of my previous occupation.'

John eventually found work as a campaigns manager for the welfare rights section of Derbyshire County Council, before standing for election to Chesterfield Council 'I got elected and within three years became leader of the council. Whether that says

I were capable or a fool, history will write I suppose. In that period of time, because leader of the council is a full time job in itself, I packed in my paid work at the county council. After the election, when we lost Chesterfield to the Lib Dems, I lost the leader's job. I'm now leader of the opposition group.'

Terry Butkeraitis found himself an industrial gypsy. Although he'd been sacked during the '84 strike, he did get his job back. He explained, 'We'd got six sacked miners at Whitwell, and some at Cresswell, and the Coal Board started industrial blackmail on us to get the jobs back. In return for taking one or two men back they demanded different shift patterns, less men working here or there, which just meant harder work for everybody.' When Whitwell colliery closed in 1989, he moved on to another North Derbyshire pit, High Moor. However, there were soon redundancies there and he was told that the policy was last in, first out. 'So if I didn't take what was on offer, I'd get nowt. There were nowhere to go after that.'

Terry found an unusual, even unique, answer to his work situation, not just for himself but for a number of his ex-mining Derbyshire colleagues in the same position. 'The people I'd met in the strike in 1984, these bike riders from London, I actually kept in touch with them to the extent that we worked for them. We helped them set up a company called the Workers Beer Company. That became the biggest provider of beer in the country at outdoor events, including Glastonbury, Reading, Leeds, all your major festivals. Then five years ago, we started Clause IV Ltd (named after the clause in the Labour Party constitution rewritten by Tony Blair which effectively separated Old Labour from New Labour). We were doing all this work for the Workers Beer Company, and we saw a niche in the market, organising events to help trade unionists. I realised that the press had manipulated me in the strike, so I thought it's pay back time, we could help by getting to manipulate the press. We do about ten stunts a year. We marched a pig into the AGM of British Gas, to draw attention to the fact that 10,000 workers had been sacked to provide a good dividend for the shareholders. Another time, after Tony Blair had called the trade unions 'the wreckers', we turned up at the Labour Party conference with a wrecking ball with posters on it, pointing out the real wreckers. NATFE, the lecturers' union, wanted to point out that the vice-chancellors had awarded themselves a 25% pay rise, while offering lecturers 2½%. The press wasn't interested until we turned up dressed as fat cats. Our logo is a miners' mole coming out of the hole wearing a miners' pit hat.'

Terry Butkeraitis certainly found a whole new life after being a coal miner, a way that combines political activity with making a living. Walter Burrows went into conventional politics after he retired as a deputy at Markham pit. He became a county councillor but was too modest to mention until I was leaving his house that I should ring before coming back to see him because he was quite busy as Chairman of Derbyshire County Council!

Paul Liversuch told me, 'When the pits shut I had the dilemma of whether I moved to another coalfield. My first instinct was to, but at the time I'd got a son getting married and another son going to university, so I decided to accept redundancy and find another job round here. I worked for an industrial cleaning firm, then I worked at a quarry until that closed down. Then I had a year out of work, and it seemed every time something came up, somebody shut the door, because they saw me as militant. They'd heard of me, my legacy had followed me round, but I'm not ashamed of being a trade unionist, I'm proud of it. Eventually I got another job industrial cleaning in Swadlincote, and even managed to start a branch of the T&G there, though the firm wouldn't recognise it. Then that firm got taken over by an American firm and I was made redundant. I did agency work for two years but I'm now doing a regular job in grounds maintenance.' As well as his actual job, and work he still does for NUM ex-miners, Paul is also very active in politics. After the strike he joined the Socialist Labour Party (president Arthur Scargill). Paul is a member of its national executive and has stood locally both as a parliamentary candidate and for the European parliament.

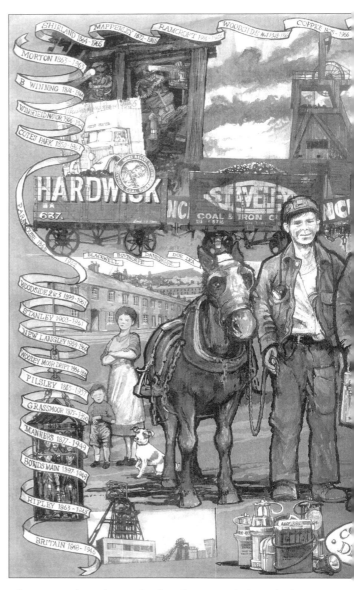

This picture by John Michael Webster entitled 'End of an Era' epitomises the life of a Derbyshire miner

That these are exceptional men there is no doubt, but their experiences of prejudice and job-hunting echo those of many ex-miners in Derbyshire after the pit closures of the 1980s and 1990s. But their memories of the mines and the mining communities from which they came still burn bright, and a new generation is growing up in the county who are coming to understand and respect the work of the Derbyshire miners.

Bibliography

100 Years of Progress, Cliff Williams (Derbyshire NUM, 1980)

Pitful of Memories: Chesterfield Teenagers Mine the Memories of a Dying Breed (St Augustine's Church 1995)

Mining In The East Midlands 1550-1947, A.R. Griffin (Cass & Co 1971)

Routes to your Roots, Alison Henesey (National Coal Mining Museum for England, 2004)

Industrial Landscapes in the East Midlands, Marilyn Palmer & Peter Neaverson (Phillimore, 1992)

Cresswell and its Mine, Barry Vardy (Minerva Press, 1998)

South Derbyshire & Its People, Oswald Hull (Derbyshire County Council, 2004)

Stitches in Time, ed Esther Davis & Julie Holdway (People Express, 1994)

The Colliers Tale, Kevin Thompson (Reid-Thompson Publishing, 1991)

Mines of Ticknall and Staunton Harold (Ticknall Preservation & Historical Society, 1999)

The Miners, R. Page Arnot (Allen & Unwin, 1952)

The Leicestershire and South Derbyshire Miners 1840-1914, Colin Griffin (NUM Leicester Area, 1981)

The Leicestershire and South Derbyshire Coalfield 1200-1900, Colin Owen (Moorlands Pub Ltd, 1984)

The Development of Industry in the South Derbyshire Coalfield, David Orme (1974)

Index

124